CHAUTAUQUA GHOSTS

Paul Leone

Chautauqua Region Press
Westfield, New York
1997

Cover: Scene near the Chadakoin River which flows out of Chautauqua Lake near Jamestown, New York. From Chautauqua County Art Work, 1893. Map from Asher and Adams Atlas of New York, circa 1869.

Library of Congress
Catalog Card No. 95-95290

ISBN 0-9658955-1-3

PRINTED IN THE UNITED STATES OF AMERICA

for

Emily Jeannette Bissell Leone

Whose Spirit Will Abide

FOREWORD

A peculiar nineteenth century ambience pervades the subtle physical beauty of Chautauqua County. The past lingers among its remote hills and isolated farms. Large tracts of wood, remnants of the unbroken forest that not so long ago covered this land, bear witness to the struggle and passion of a self assured ancestry. They were men and women of strong conviction. Their spirit remains. The history of Chautauqua County is accessible. It continues to unfold in the letters and journals, documents and artifacts, that so regularly surface in these isolated farmhouses and still intact Victorian villages. That the citizenry of this land is still largely descended from its earliest residents has much to do with the ambience. Chautauqua County remains a place one is likely to have been born to. Those who revere the journals and documents, and the spirit of their antecedents, often inhabit the very premises of those antecedents. Such continuity contributes to defining this community.

I am often asked by schoolchildren whether or not I believe in ghosts. I always answer that ghosts exist for those who wish them to exist. That is not to say that a ghost is, necessarily, an incorporeal being. To one fascinated and inspired by the stories of individuals, a ghost may be the result of a conscious act or choice, or the mere memory of the result. One's choices affect a sphere wider than oneself. The effects of passion often remain after the passion is gone. Mother love protects even beyond the mother's grave. Betrayal returns to haunt betrayer as well as betrayed.

Memories, it seems to me, age well. A ghost story, like history, ought to have some age to it. Seven of the eight stories in this volume touch the Victorian years. Those years were at once colorful and energetic, sleepy and formal. The strict Victorian code of conduct is today every bit as other worldly as a ghost. Passion conflicted with Victorian rectitude either for good or for evil. Chautauqua ghosts return for a reason: to right a wrong, to protect a loved one, to complete unfinished work, to help those left behind to remember.

Most of the stories in "Chautauqua Ghosts" begin with place. Most of the settings are distinct and will be immediately identifiable to Chautauquans. "Daniel Kenton" and "Dayton's Ghost" cross the border into Cattaraugus County. Genuine historical figures appear alongside the creations of my imagination. The line between fact and fantasy is thin. Each story is introduced with a brief word on its conception. The work is designed to celebrate the region called Chautauqua. May it long continue as it is.

To the many whose support and encouragement made this volume possible, I express my sincere thanks: to Pat White for her interest in this and all my other storytelling endeavors; to Martha Lindner and Mary Tangelos for their recommendations for funding to the Fund for the Arts in Chautauqua County; and to the Fund for the Arts for its 1995 fellowship grant to aid in printing costs. I should also like to thank the Fenton Historical Museum for the use of its resources and the Council on the Arts in Chautauqua County for its professionalism and dedication in administering local programs relating to the Arts.

For her critical eye and helpful suggestions thanks to Ann Servoss.

For her technical help thanks to Elaine LaMattina of White Pine Press, Fredonia.

And, finally, a very warm thanks to Don Dankert with whom I spent a delightful afternoon exploring the vicinity of Norton's Station for the story "Joseph Damon and His Wife"; and to Devon Taylor, Mayville town historian, for making me aware of the invitation to the hanging that introduces that story; to Joyce La Judice, National Spiritualists' Association archivist at Lily Dale for the use of her wonderful archives; and to Barbara Ferraro for her explication of the tenets of Spiritualism.

PML
November 1, 1995

CONTENTS

Joseph Damon and His Wife 1

Mary Peabody 13

Prudence and Charity Chatham 21

Allen's Opera House 27

Alva Lazell 33

Dayton's Ghost 41

Panama Rocks 47

Daniel Kenton 71

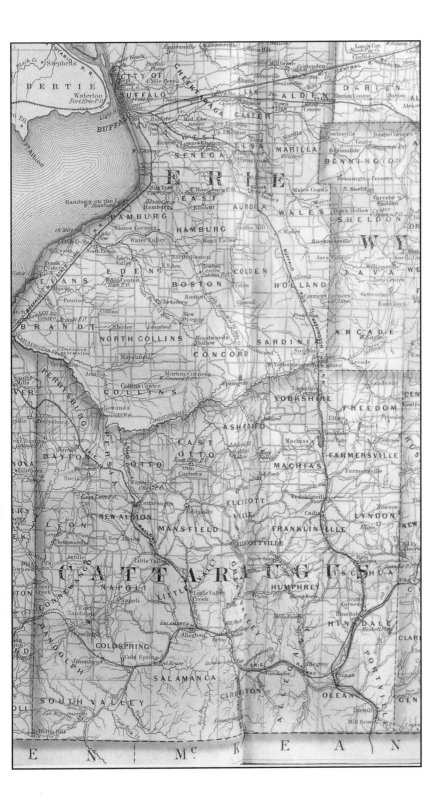

E.T. Foote Esquire First Judge of County Courts

Per fin I intended to have seen you at Mayville before the boat started for Jamestown but did not arrive in season. I hope you will attend and witness the Execution of Joseph Damon which is to take place on the 15th inst. and be here at 9 o'clock in the morning in order to walk in the procession.

Your compliance with the above request will grately oblige your humble Servant.

William Sexton Sheff
Mayville May 12th 1835

The original of this note sent to Judge Foote by William Sexton remains in the Mayville historical archives under the care of Devon Taylor. Joseph Damon's was the last public execution to be held in New York state. Damon was hanged three days after the note was sent in the little village of Mayville, the county seat, for the murder of his wife. Newspapers estimated the crowd in attendance at about ten thousand, or a quarter of the county population. Mrs. Damon's Christian name was never referred to in the newspaper accounts of the murder and trial. County histories identify Sheriff William Sexton as "Sheriff Saxton", and so he remains in the following story. Solomon Porter is fictional. Casey's Hotel survives as the Old Corner Deli in Hartfield.

Joseph Damon and His Wife

Yes, sir. I heard them voices. I never did see Damon, though. Not after the hangin'. Didn't half believe anyone said they saw him. Leastways, not till I started hearin' them voices. Now, I don't know. I heard them voices plenty a times. Always on over to Norton's Station. Always on the evenin' run. Soundin' like they were far off on the wind. Folks're still hearin' 'em. Railroaders, mostly. Course not like they used to after the accident. You know about the accident? Killed the boy over to Norton's Station? Train run over him. Folks started listenin' then. Soundin' like a man cursin', a woman prayin'. You might hear one one night an' the other another. I heard 'em both sometimes. That accident stirred 'em up. Got folks to seein' Damon again, too. Not around here. Over to Mayville. Soon's they heard about the accident seems like old Damon started showin' up again. You know where the schoolhouse is over to Mayville? That's where they saw him. That's where they hung him. I never knew anyone saw him around here. After they hung him, I mean. I sometimes wished I would'a seen him, just to know if it was true. Would'a been awful frightenin' now, wouldn't it? Them voices are frightenin' enough. I ain't heard 'em for a while now. Not since I stopped railroadin'. I always hear about 'em, though. When they get riled up. The new boys come to tell me. I tell 'em what I know.

Solomon Porter, in his retirement, was the acknowledged authority on the matter of the Damons. This ill fated family, not one of whom was personally known to Solomon Porter, had occupied his attention

3

and, indeed, the attention of the entire county for more than three score years. Periodic reportings by railroad men of mysterious voices in the vicinity of Norton's Station continued throughout Solomon Porter's lifetime. The reports awakened in the county a collective memory of events sooner forgotten. Whenever the voices were heard, Solomon Porter was consulted. He had been present at the very beginning. He had witnessed the fatal accident, at Norton's Station, whose implications so shocked the county. And, what's more, he claimed to have heard the voices himself, many times, even before the accident.

Solomon Porter collected tickets on the old Dunkirk, Allegheny Valley, and Pittsburg Railroad in its early days. The D.A.V. and P.R.R. ran south through the rich agricultural land of Chautauqua County to its terminus at Titusville. It commenced operations in 1871 and during its lifetime provided reliable passenger service, as well as Pennsylvania coal, lumber, and oil, to the citizens of Dunkirk. Three miles below Fredonia, in the town of Pomfret, the tracks paralleled the old Chautauqua Road. Beyond Norton's Station they curved east and followed the creek bed of the Little Canadaway close to Damon's Quarry. This was land that then belonged to Elisha Norton.

It was still called Damon's Quarry, although by then the Damons were long gone. Solomon Porter used to like to point it out to his passengers. He also pointed out what was left of the two wooden houses the Damons had lived in, the one occupied by the elder Mr. and Mrs. Damon and their oldest son Martin, the other by Joseph Damon and his family. That was the house, Solomon Porter said, in emphatic tones, where Joseph Damon bludgeoned his wife to death with an iron fire poker. They hung him for it, he told the solemn, listening faces.

4

Right there on that hill over to Mayville. Behind the schoolhouse. And any among his passengers who remembered nodded.

The passengers listened with faces set, especially after the accident. The accident awakened the collective memory, only fitfully slumbering even after almost forty years. What happened there at Norton's Station, what might have happened there, bore on their own place in the universe. When he had told them enough, Solomon Porter directed them to listen. *Listen for a curse*, he told them. *Listen for a prayer.*

Solomon Porter, in his retirement, considered carefully any reports from Norton's Station. The crew of the D.A.V. and P.R.R. was new and unreliable. What they had or had not been hearing out there could never be verified. Nevertheless, whenever they asked, he told them what he knew. What Solomon Porter knew, in his heart of hearts, was that something about the Damons remained. He was an old man now. But his memory was sharp. He was one of the last who really remembered. He had been there at the hanging.

Joseph Damon was a strong man, hard muscled after years of pulling out the rock that his brother Martin chiseled into gravestones. They said at his trial he was passionate and given to drink, although not one of the witnesses had ever seen him drunk. Mr. James Mullett, Esq., celebrated attorney for the defense, maintained that he was prone to fits of delirium, that he was deranged when he committed the crime. His mother testified that she feared the look in his eyes as he left her house that afternoon.

He was unrepentant. Through a year of incarceration in the newly built jail, among the hemlocks, he expected acquittal. Even on the gallows he showed no remorse. With the rope about his neck he protested, passionately, that he had acted in self defense.

It was a May morning. The sun was shining. The open hillside was covered with the thousands who had come to watch. Some had been there three days, camping under their wagons, horses grazing at the edge of the wood line, women and children, too. There was little pity. Who could pity this strong and brutal man, unremorseful, who had bloodied and beaten until she was dead his wife and the mother of his children? His wife had a weak constitution, they said. His children, Nancy, age eleven, and John, two years younger, were standing in the dooryard. Everyone knew he had ordered them there. Everyone knew all about Joseph Damon. The whole county knew, after the trial was over. He had come in to the house, eyes blazing, and ordered them out to the dooryard to pick up the wood chips he had dropped from a load of firewood he had brought up that afternoon. And then, when they were gone, he had beaten their mother to death. They heard their mother's cries. They heard her pleading, not for herself, but for their sake. The sleeve of her dress was ripped, and there were gashes in her arm where she had tried to fend off his blows. She had four deep wounds in her skull, any one of which would have killed her. They saw her lying in her blood on the floor of her house.

He was an unbeliever. That was what had crazed him. That his wife insisted on going to meeting and reading her bible in spite of him; and more than that, that his mother and father and brother Martin upheld her. When he left his mother's house that afternoon, after yet another argument, as he crossed the street to his own, his mother feared the look in his eyes.

Elder Sawyer preached his funeral sermon. He preached from Proverbs: He that pursueth evil, pursueth it to his own death. Those that had come to watch listened; and after the drop fell, with its awful sound, they stood aghast, unbelieving, for the fastenings had slipped, and Joseph Damon was not swinging in the spring air but lying dazed on the hillside, the noose swaying empty above him.

He maintained that the judgement had been carried out and that the state now had no right to him. He protested, passionately, anger again rising to his eyes, as he realized they were going to hang him twice. And now the eyes betrayed his fear as well. Perhaps a few among the thousands felt a stir of compassion; but more were restless and impatient. Voices shouted out to get the work done. Sheriff Saxton, grim and implacable, fixed the rope again about the neck of Joseph Damon, still protesting. In the brief, expectant moment before the drop fell a second time, the hillside was quiet. Perhaps the wind stirred among the hemlocks. The horses stood still in their traces. This time, at the dreadful sound of the drop, Joseph Damon was hurtled into his eternity. *He that pursueth evil, pursueth it to his own death.*

Self-defense? said Solomon Porter. *No. But I'll tell you what I think. I think Mr. Mullett was right. He was crazy. He was crazy on that gallows that second time. Can you imagine? All those people watching? He swore he didn't know what he was doing. Said he couldn't remember nothin' about it at all. He didn't stop talking once while that sheriff was fixin' that rope. I never saw a man so scared. I saw him good. I was close. He was crazy all right.*

Martin Damon never fashioned his brother's stone. The state was not finished with him, it appears, for no one of his family ever claimed the body. No

7

Damon attended the execution. The corpse was taken in a buckboard to Casey's Hotel in Hartfield where it remained through the night and into the following day. The authorities sent word to Martin asking what he wished for the body. Martin said that neither he nor any member of his family wanted anything to do with it. Joseph Damon was buried at the expense of the county; and that should have been that. The matter refused to rest with his body, however. Six months after the hanging Sheriff Saxton turned up missing. Then, within the year, Martin Damon fell to his death in the quarry.

No one doubted that the sheriff's disappearance was related to the hanging. The sheriff had been intimately involved with the proceedings from the beginning, and Damon's body was entrusted to his care upon its removal from Casey's Hotel. The sheriff's friends and colleagues were well aware that he hadn't been the same from the time of the hanging. He held himself responsible for the failed first attempt. The disappearance was thoroughly investigated. His neighbors said he had talked of moving away to Canada. If so, he left without a trace.

The unfortunate Mrs. Damon found Martin's body on a wet April morning at the bottom of the quarry. The coroner ruled the death accidental. Some sort of attack, the coroner believed, for Martin had had a weak heart. What he had been doing out there on a rainy night, Mrs. Damon could not say.

Mr. James Mullett, Esq., whose professional and personal conduct in relation to the Damons continued exemplary, paid the surviving parents a visit of condolence. He found them in a fearful state. They said they had been awakened several nights running by the sound of angry voices coming from Joseph's house. Although she hadn't told the coroner, Mrs. Damon admitted to Mr. Mullett that she had heard the voices the night of

Martin's death. The house had been empty since the hanging. They had seen no one.

Mr. Mullett examined the house and its surroundings but found no sign of intruders. He used his influence to secure a place for the Damons in the county poor farm where they lived out the rest of their lives.

You know what he did find? The wife's bible. He told Old Man Casey. You know Old Man Casey? Run the hotel over to Hartfield? Where they took the body after the hangin'? He was runnin' it then, too. Mr. Mullett told him it give him a creepy feeling seein' that bible lyin' there on the wife's rockin' chair. Like she was still plaguin' him. Old Man Casey was one of them said he saw Damon. I don't know about that. After the hangin' folks was always claimin' they'd seen him. Still do, sometimes. You know how folks talk. They got to sayin' maybe he wasn't dead. Maybe he killed the sheriff and got away. Old Man Casey saw him twice. Said he was carryin' that fire poker. Now what do you suppose happened to that fire poker? That sheriff had it with him when he took the body away. I never did half believe 'em. I remember them Harkness boys, though. I hayed for their pa. You don't know about them. First ones to hear the voices, I reckon, not countin' Mr. and Mrs. Damon. After the accident I'd'a believed anything. Old Man Casey was always scared to be alone in that hotel. Go on over there and see it. It's still standin'. Well, I never did see Damon. But I heard them voices plenty. I'll tell you one thing, though; if I'd'a seen him, I'd'a known him. You don't forget a hangin'.

The first time John Casey saw Joseph Damon–the first time he saw him after he saw him dead–he was shutting down for the evening. His guests had gone to bed.

Stepping out onto the porch, he noticed a figure standing in the shadows on the opposite side of the road. It was half moonlight, and at first he thought it must be one of the guests, the one who had been drinking heavily. He never thought then it was Damon. When he called, the figure moved off. The guest in question was sound asleep.

Mr. Mullett, stopping at the hotel a few days later for lunch, told Casey about the "fool talk" going on over in Mayville. Three separate witnesses were saying they had seen Damon in the darkness on the hillside where he had been hanged.

Mr. Mullett judged it all nonsense. The witnesses had made the claim on the very day of the anniversary of the hanging. All year long the talk in the county had been of nothing but that dismal event. No one had yet seen the missing sheriff; and Martin Damon's death was causing speculation. That time John Casey didn't tell Mr. Mullett what he had seen.

Then the Harkness boys found the fire poker; and heard the voices. Thirteen year old Jacob said it was lying in the brush at the edge of the quarry and that his brother North had actually held it in his hands. Two deaths and a hanging had given the area a considerable reputation, and the Harkness boys had gone there on a dare from their comrades. Mr. and Mrs. Damon were gone. Jacob said that the two boys had actually entered Joseph Damon's house. When they realized what they had found, they panicked and began to run. The man cursed, Jacob said. The woman was praying. Both of them heard.

Bill Harkness, the boys' father, notified Sheriff Gates. He insisted on accompanying the sheriff to investigate, and he insisted that his boys go along. The house, empty now of furniture, appeared undisturbed. The fire poker was gone.

*She wasn't exactly prayin', I don't guess. She
was readin' the bible. That's what I heard. I heard the
cursin', too. He didn't like it at all. Killed her for it.
Mr. Mullett was right. That fire poker never did show up
that I know of. 'Cept folks that saw Damon said he was
carryin' it. Old Casey said he had it the second time.
The bible neither. Not after Mr. Mullett saw it. Thieves
could'a got it, I suppose. They took everything else was-
n't nailed down. But that young woman was there the
night of the accident?–she had a bible. Leastways that's
what them ladies who saw her said. I never saw her.
Hadley did. That's our engineer. He's dead now. Said
he thought she was waitin' for a ride. Always stopped
for passengers, Hadley did. Them ladies said one sleeve
of her dress was all tore up, and her arm was bloody.
She wasn't waitin' for no ride. She never got on the
train. Hadley even got down to look for her. Seemed
like she just disappeared. The boy was drunk alright. I
knew that. Wasn't unusual comin' up from the oil country. He wasn't supposed to get off the train. Might be
he recognized the young woman. It was most dark.
There's a blind spot out there. Worse now that it's all
growed up. Hadley just backed over him. Wasn't his
fault. Nothin' we could do but bring the body on into
Dunkirk. He didn't have no identification. Had a lot of
money in his pocket. We didn't find out who he was till
later. Lord God Almighty–John Damon.*

Solomon Porter is long gone, and Norton's
Station, too, and the D.A.V. and P.R.R. But the track
bed along the old Chautauqua Road is intact. In the
woods beyond Kasbohm's Poultry Farm you can still find
the ties. The creek bed of the Little Canadaway is filled

with quarry slate. The young boys who live in the few houses along old Chautauqua Road ride their four wheelers on the track bed. Solomon Porter would have warned them to stop and listen. To stop behind Kasbohm's, where Norton's Station was. *Listen for a curse. Listen for a prayer.*

The hill on which stands the Central School in Mayville, across the street from the courthouse and the county jail, has been leveled half way down to make room for an athletic field. The undersheriff's wife, who teaches there, is uneasy, alone in the evening, in the school building. Outside, in the darkness, halfway down the hill, it might be that Joseph Damon is leaning on his fire poker. The thousands who were there are watching. All, all are looking toward the stars, above the goal posts, very much like a gallows.

In the summer of 1862 William Depledge enlisted into Company G of the 112th New York Volunteers, nicknamed the "Chautauqua Regiment". He left his wife Jenie and their three sons on a rented farm in Arkwright when he went off to the War. William Depledge died of fever in North Carolina one week prior to Lee's surrender. His story is poignantly told in his own hand in a collection of letters to his family written from the field of battle. The collection belongs to his great grandson, Mr. Ken Depledge, of Falconer. More than an account of William's war experience, the letters describe Jenie's struggle for survival alone on the farm. The news of her husband's death, which arrived in a letter from his unit's chaplain, must have been devastating for her. The image of Jenie with that letter in hand in my imagination was the inspiration for "Mary Peabody".

Mary Peabody

Hiram Green and his wife Margaret ran the general store in the little country village of Arkwright in the days before the Civil War. Hiram was an old man, and Margaret was old, too, and they had been keeping that store for so long that most everybody around Arkwight knew them. Folks knew Hiram and Margaret both to be kind and gentle people and honest as the day was long. The two of them loved the young men and women who'd come out to the county to try and make a living out of farming, growing wheat. Hiram was always willing to extend the young farmers credit, and he was never quick to demand his money when they couldn't pay. The older gents used to chuckle, and Doc Weatherall told Hiram he was getting old, losing his memory, when he forgot what this or that young man owed him. But Hiram always seemed to forget just when the young man was seeing hard times. And when the young men and women began to have families, and children came along, Margaret always gave to them one of the fine warm quilts she pieced together at night after the store was closed. Hiram and Margaret spent the cold evenings of fall in the store where they would stoke up the wood stove; and Margaret would sit sewing, and Hiram would tidy up, then sit down himself and light up his pipe. Hiram and Margaret never had any children of their own.

One of the young couples they looked out for had newly arrived and rented a farm some miles out in the countryside. The young man's name was Jefferson. Jefferson Peabody. He was strong and rugged and full of energy. His wife's name was Mary; and she, too, was strong and determined, willing to work. They hadn't been out there more than a year or two when the War came along. And when the War came, there was great excitement all over the county. Seemed like the young men couldn't wait to join up. Speeches were given and money was raised and those young farmers found out just how patriotic they were. And then, the young men began to leave. Jefferson Peabody was one of them. He left Mary at home on the farm. He told her how the army would pay him well, two hundred and fifty dollars cash just for signing up; and when he returned, they would give him land, a farm of their own. Mary could see there was no stopping him, so she gave her consent. And then, Jefferson was gone. It wasn't long after Mary realized she was with child.

Jefferson Peabody never did return from the War. The letter said he fought bravely and was well respected by both the officers and the men. He died at a place called Antietam. Mary received in the mail his uniform and the money that was due him. The way Mary figured it, he died about the time his child was being born.

She called the child Felicity, because it brought joy to her heart. Brown skinned, she was, like her Mama, and blue eyed and healthy. The first thing Hiram and Margaret did was to try and talk Mary into bringing the child with her into the village to live with them in their house behind the store. Mary wouldn't hear of it. She said she meant to buy the farm with the money left her at Jefferson's death. "It's what we always aimed to do," she said. "Lord willin'. And I ain't going to change it now." Margaret gave Felicity the quilt with the red and blue flannel patches, and Hiram built her a crib. And Hiram insisted on driving out to the farm day after day until he had the wood laid in for the winter that was approaching.

Winter was early that year, '62 it was. The snow began to blow up in November. Mary came in to the store once a week, Saturday afternoons, regular as clock-work, for her flour and sugar. Bundled up that child Felicity in the red and blue quilt, fixed up a riding seat for her in the wagon, and come on in. Hiram said she worked that mule good as any man. As the days went on Hiram made one excuse after another to ride out to the farm to see how things were getting on. He'd take Mary some apples or summer preserves and see how the wood was holding out. Told Margaret when he came back, sitting around that wood stove smoking his pipe, told her how the fire was always up and the house was warm; and most always there was bread baking in the oven, the mule was fed, and the child Felicity lay in the crib sleeping or looking around, wrapped in the red and blue quilt. Told her how sometimes he took the child on his knee and it looked up into his face.

"That's a proud woman," he told Margaret.

And Margaret nodded.

After the new year the winter set in hard. The weather dropped and folks held up inside for four and five days. Mary didn't show up at the store that Saturday. Come Sunday Hiram wanted to ride out to see was she all right. Margaret said he oughtn't to do that. Hiram was an old man, and he oughtn't to be out in weather like that.

Two days later she appeared. It was just after sundown, and Hiram and Margaret were sitting by the fire in the light of candles. They heard the wagon pull up, and then there was a knock on the door. When Hiram opened it, there stood Mary. She came in quick, followed by a cold wind. And then, Margaret was on her feet, telling Mary to come to the fire and warm herself. But Mary only spoke, quickly, "Please, I need milk for the child." In the dim light of the candles Margaret could see the anxious look on her face. "Are you ill, Mary?"

"No, but I must hurry. The child is alone." Hiram went to the back room and brought out a little clear bottle of milk, handed it to Mary, and almost before they knew it, she was gone and they could hear the creaking of the wagon as it went off into the night. Margaret said to Hiram there must be trouble, for a healthy young woman like Mary didn't need no cow's milk for her child. Hiram wanted to follow, but Margaret said he best wait till morning.

The next day a storm blew up. The snow flew around thick and covered the country. Hiram and Margaret spent all day in the store, but no one came. Toward dark the snow finally stopped. While they were sitting down to supper, there came another knock on the door. Hiram reached it before the knocking stopped and opened to find Mary standing there in the snow. "Please, I need milk. The child needs milk."

This time Margaret began to scold. "This night ain't fittin' for man or beast. You come over here and set down by the fire. Where's your child?" But, again Mary spoke up, desperate. "Hurry. The child is alone." And, again, Hiram went for the little glass bottle and she vanished out the door.

The next day Hiram was hitching up the team, bound and determined to go out to the farm and bring back Mary and the child to stay for the rest of the winter. The weather had broken some, but while he was climbing into the wagon, Hiram slipped and fell to the ground and banged up his leg pretty bad. Margaret had an awful time getting him back into the store, and then she had to run off and fetch Doc Weatherall, and by the time they got back and the Doc got Hiram patched up it was getting dark. Margaret said he could go in the morning and she'd go out there with him. But while they were readying up for bed, there came that knock on the door and

Mary came in again, hurrying and out of breath.
"Please, the child is alone." Hiram limped off after the
milk, and when he handed it to her this time, he noticed
a bruise on the side of her forehead. He wanted to run
off and fetch Doc Weatherall back, but she was out the
door before him. When he looked out after her, she was
gone, no sign of a wagon at all, just the silence of the
night. So he called out into the dark, "Ye'll be comin' in
tomorrow for the winter."

Neither Margaret nor Hiram slept much that
night. In the morning they were up quick and dressed
and together they got the team hitched up and Margaret
helped Hiram into the wagon, and they were on their
way. The sun was out, and it was going to be warmer.
When they reached the farm, they could see smoke rising
from the chimney. And before they knocked, they could
hear the sound of Mary's voice talking low to the child
and singing. The voice answered their knock in the same
quiet tone. "It's open."

She stood up when they entered. She had been
feeding the child from that third bottle, and it was almost
empty now. She smiled at them, standing there holding
the almost empty bottle; and Margaret remembered afterwards the other two bottles were setting on the wallshelf
behind the stove, clean and dry, and there was a tin pot
on the burner with water in it to heat the milk. The
bruise on her forehead stood out clearer now. She continued to smile. And although Hiram and Margaret had
prepared to be angry with her, they found they could not
speak.

"Thank you for coming." She was smiling still.
"Please, sit down." She lifted the child out of her crib
and handed her to Margaret along with the bottle of milk.
"Would you mind?" Then she asked if they could wait
while she saw to the mule. When she reached the door,

she turned to them and smiled once more. "Goodbye."

They waited for what seemed a long time, but she didn't return. Finally, Hiram lost his patience and got up and limped out to the barn to see what was keeping her. Out at the barn there wasn't a sound. He called out, "Mary!" but there was no answer. When he went inside, he saw the mule first, standing in its stall, quiet. And below the stall, lying in the hay, there was a woman's body. He went to her and looked down on her face, which was white now, and on the side of her forehead there was a deep gash in the shape of a mule's hoof. It was Mary. She was dead.

Doc Weatherall said she'd been dead for more than a week. Hiram and Margaret carried her to the wagon. They wrapped up the child Felicity in the red and blue flannel quilt and loaded up the crib. Then they drove back to the store. Preacher said a few words, and they carried the body back to the farm where they buried it. Hiram and Margaret raised up the child Felicity til she was a grown woman, and then they could die. Felicity bought that farm and run it for a good many years, and made it pay, too. She had a whole passel of children of her own. And now most of them are buried up there on the farm with their grandmother; and their children, too. On the marker in the middle of them, Mary's marker, you can still make out Hiram's words, "That's a Proud Woman".

*The idea for "Prudence and Charity Chatham"
germinated in the remarks of a fourth grade student
at Panama Central School. After a presentation
of ghost stories one recent Halloween, I was visit-
ing individual classrooms to discuss with the children their experiences with ghosts. A fervent
young lady insisted she had knowledge of two elder-
ly sisters living together, one of whom was dead. I
found the suggestion entirely plausible and utterly
delightful. The two sisters, I was sure, were digni-
fied and refined like my own great Aunt Jo, whose
spirit certainly remains with us. In order to
strengthen the physical bond between them, I made
them twins. The story is set in Ashville, because
that pretty little village, at once secluded and accessible, seems to me worthy of two such ladies. All
of the characters save one are fictional. Most read-
ers will recognize the single historical figure off-
handedly mentioned in the story.*

Prudence and Charity Chatham

A venerable, red brick house graces the silent and shady streets of the little village of Ashville. The house bespeaks a quiet dignity. It rises on a slight hill behind a grove of white oak and the narrow overgrown banks of a creek whose name is now forgotten. The gardens behind are visible, too, brilliant in summer with hosts of purple irises, lilies, and magnificent roses. Passersby sometimes pause before the Chatham house to gaze upon it and its lovely yard. The Chathams are gone now, and their memory is fading; but there are still some who remember the sisters Prudence and Charity, who seem to see them yet through the trunks of the oaks, among their beautiful flowers, Prudence in her wheelchair and straw hat and Charity at her side. The house is lovingly kept by its present owners. The flowers bloom each year in splendor, faithful to the love ever bestowed upon them.

The Misses Prudence and Charity Chatham, twins, were the youngest of the nine children born to Thomas and Penelope Chatham. Thomas Chatham was among the first in the county to cash in on the trade in potash and pearl ash for which the little village was named. He came out from Framingham in Massachusetts in the year 1819, lured by a pioneer spirit and the promise of cheap land. Already, the forest was being cut to make way for farms. Mr. Chatham bought up as much as he could of the hardwood ash left after the farmers burned their fallen trees. He built his first ashery at the age of twenty-three. The product of his kilns fueled the glass factories of Pittsburgh and cleansed the shorn wool that fed England's ravenous textile mills. In three years time he had a second ashery and the beginnings of a general store, too, where ash could be traded and cash avoided.

His was one of Chautauqua's first brick houses.
Prudence and Charity were born in that house when
Thomas Chatham was sixty years old.

Hardly before they were grown their brothers and sisters were gone. And most of the nieces and nephews
that were their playmates in their youth. Only Charles
Chatham remained, the son of Ephraim, a retired banker
who had survived the crash. He was three years older
than his aunts. Mr. Charles Chatham saw it coming. He
had been a shrewd businessman and knew well the
effects of out of control lending and speculation. Shortly
after Mr. Hoover's election, he redeemed his securities
and invested with Barclay's of London. He lived in
Buffalo. His aunts visited him there once a year.

Neither sister ever married. Not that they hadn't had
chances. Charity was actually engaged while at college.
The two attended Elmira and turned heads wherever they
appeared. They were tall and erect then, beautiful young
women filled with the promise of life. They excelled at
their studies. The young man was a friend of Mr.
Clemens. At parties Mr. Clemens used to like to escort
the two sisters, one on each arm, to the table. The
engagement was broken off immediately after graduation.
Charity's fiance, it turned out, had been carrying on all
along a secret and scandalous liaison. There had been a
scene. Prudence and Charity returned to Ashville. The
young man pursued in great despair. He pleaded to deaf
ears, however, and finally departed, ignominiously.

Thomas Chatham died the following year. Penelope
suffered from a debilitating bone disease that frequently
left her immobile. Prudence and Charity watched over
their mother and kept her company until her death five
years later. With their inheritance they opened a progressive school for girls that in time earned an enviable reputation. Prudence spoke out publicly for women's rights

and against the abuse of alcohol. The two became quite fashionable. Each entertained an occasional romance, but their dedication to work and to each other always interfered. Before she was old Prudence began to show signs of her mother's illness. Eventually, she was confined to a wheelchair. Charity administered the school alone until her sister was no longer able to manage without her. For the rest of their lives the two lived in tranquil retirement in the red brick house. Summers they spent in their magnificent gardens, and in the fall they made their yearly trip to visit Charles.

The events surrounding Prudence's death occasioned much talk and speculation and some concern among those who were privy to them. The story grew in proportion over the years and eventually achieved the status of legend. Of the few left today who remember Miss Prudence and Miss Charity, however, there are fewer still willing to discuss with any seriousness those events. The best authority on the subject is John Wickham, who still lives in Ashville. Mr. Wickham's father, Seth Wickham, used to deliver groceries to the Misses Chatham in their retirement. John was a schoolboy then. He remembers that his father held the two sisters in the highest esteem. All his long life Seth Wickham spoke lovingly of Miss Prudence and Miss Charity. He considered it an honor to have known them and never once felt the slightest anxiety in their presence. Miss Prudence invited him in for tea the winter Miss Charity stayed over in Buffalo. Seth Wickham was forever very fond of Bertha May, the big red headed woman who returned from Buffalo with Miss Prudence that winter.

It was the winter of '32 according to Old Selstrom. Old Selstrom was certain, for the country was celebrating Mr. Roosevelt's election. It was he–Old Selstrom, a young man then, of course–who had driven Miss

Prudence and Bertha May home from the depot. Old Selstrom remembered that Bertha May had had considerable luggage. He also remembered, clearly, having asked after Miss Charity. Miss Prudence told him Miss Charity would be along directly.

John Wickham says his father took great pride in having been among the first to greet Miss Charity upon her return. Seth Wickham was out to the house in the spring not two days after Miss Charity's arrival. He lunched with Miss Prudence and Miss Charity and Bertha May in the garden. In the years that followed the teas continued. Sometimes, Seth Wickham said, the sisters insisted that he sing. Miss Prudence played the piano from her wheelchair, and he and Miss Charity sang duets. Miss Charity said he had a beautiful tenor voice. Seth Wickham notified Mr. Charles when Miss Prudence died.

Everyone agreed that Mr. Charles was very distinguished. Mr. Charles had been returning his aunts' visits for some time. He always came the second week of August and stayed precisely eight days. Mrs. Compton said he had been coming for six years. Mrs. Compton was friendly with Bertha May, and she knew. She remembered because she had admired Mr. Charles' new black Cadillac car and his handsome driver, too. The first time Mr. Charles came was the year Mr. Roosevelt closed the banks. And, Seth Wickham pointed out, it must have been the year after Bertha May and not Miss Charity returned from Buffalo with Miss Prudence. Mr. Charles loved Mrs. Compton's peach preserves. Mrs. Compton took him a jar every year. Seth Wickham liked them, too. Seth Wickham made much of the fact that Mrs. Compton had once told him how strange she thought it was that Miss Charity never seemed to be about when Mr. Charles visited. She also told him that

Bertha May had told her she never spoke of Miss Charity
in Mr. Charles' presence. Once, Mrs. Compton asked
after Miss Charity, and Mr. Charles looked at her with a
strange expression. Mrs. Compton always maintained
that the big Cadillac car and the driver looked every bit
as good the day of the funeral.

Miss Prudence was buried in the family plot in the
cemetery at the edge of the village. The entire village
turned out. Everyone wondered what had become of
Miss Charity. Everyone was concerned. Miss Charity
had been conspicuously absent since the evening before
when the house was full of guests. Mr. Charles respond-
ed to inquiries with much confusion. He remained at the
Chatham house for several days after the funeral. Those
who called with food and kind words reported no evidence at all of Miss Charity. No one ever saw her again.
Bertha May returned to Buffalo. Mr. Charles lived on a
number of years in vigorous good health. Upon his death
the house was acquired by the family that still occupies it.
The gardens continue to bloom each year in brilliant
color. In his will Mr. Charles inserted this provision: "In
recognition of the strong bond between them and their
mutual love the sum of five hundred dollars is provided
for the exhumation and removal to Ashville, New York of
the remains of my aunt, Miss Charity Chatham". The
marker in the Chatham plot reads:

> Charity Chatham
> Born Ashville, N.Y.
> June 12, 1859
> Died Buffalo, N.Y.
> Nov. 5, 1932
> "A Woman Kind Is a Gift From Heaven"

Allen's Opera House hosted all manner of entertainments—minstrel shows, plays, lectures, musical showcases, ventriloquist acts, masquerade balls, magic shows, etc., etc.,–throughout the last quarter of the nineteenth century. The original opera house stood on the site of what is today the Reg Lenna Civic Center at the corner of Third and Spring Streets in Jamestown. It was at that facility that the English actor Mr. Thomas Keene and his Shakespearean troupe performed, providing the basis for "Allen's Opera House". Mr. Keene's troupe performed "Macbeth", not "Hamlet". Although both plays do contain a ghost, the ghost in "Macbeth" appears in only a single scene. The plot of my story requires that the ghost leave the stage and return after an extended time. I have removed the location to Abner Allen's second opera house, a building still standing, in order to furnish our ghost with a visible haven. The staff at the Reg Lenna assure me they are quite comfortable with their own ghosts.

Allen's Opera House

Mr. Abner Elisha Allen built his second Opera House on a prominent site on East Second Street. The first burned to the ground in the winter of 1881. The little city of Jamestown was colorful and energetic then, and the business district thrived. Mr. Allen's second Opera House was, and still is, a substantial structure. It is painted a blue-grey color now. The decorative features that are left are highlighted in cream and black. Gone are the high arched windows, bricked over, and the wrought iron railings of the second story balconies, and the balconies, too. But there remains about the building a degree of Victorian stature commensurate with the progressive and smug conception the little city had of itself.

Mr. Allen's Opera House is still a house of entertainments. Today, it is the home of the Lucille Ball Little Theatre of Jamestown. It is named after the illustrious comedienne who was a child of this city. Members of the Lucille Ball Little Theatre often report strange phenomena within its walls: a chill descends upon its empty cavern, a door closes, footfalls echo off the deserted stage, late night rehearsers catch fleeting glimpses of incorporeal beings. Are these the ghosts of forgotten actors and actresses? Adulation is what they seek. Immortality. For those not satisfied in life the search continues beyond the grave.

Lucius Dascum was one such. The career of Lucius Dascum ended as tragically as the scenes he would have played had he lived to fulfill his promise. One summer's eve, when the house was full and expectation high, when all Jamestown had turned out in its carriages and its finery, while the audience sat rapt, suspended in the bliss of triumphant performance, Lucius Dascum played out his final scene on a different stage. Not thirty minutes after the performance ended Lucius Dascum was found behind the Opera House, in the street known as Potter's Alley, lying in a pool of blood. A dagger pierced his heart.

He was a member of Mr. Thomas Keene's celebrated Shakespearean troupe from London. The troupe had been engaged that night for a single performance of Hamlet. Afterwards, no one remembered having seen Mr. Dascum from the time of his last appearance in Act III. As the ghost of Hamlet's slain father he appeared briefly in Scene IV, the famous bedroom scene. Although he was on stage only a matter of minutes, his effect on the audience was profound. Reporting the murder, the Jamestown Journal remarked that this final appearance seemed to cast "a pall of dread" over the audience. Lucius Dascum spoke his few lines as if in torment. That the murder must have been committed shortly thereafter, perhaps while the play was still in progress, no doubt influenced the audience's recollection. The Journal pointed out that Lucius Dascum never made the curtain call. Everyone was certain of that. For he had played the ghost so well the audience awaited him. Nevertheless, Mr. Keene himself, playing Hamlet, recalled that at the entrance of the ghost in Act III he had felt a sudden chill, something physical, like nothing he had ever before experienced. Investigators detained the entire troupe for a matter of days. Before long they were convinced of the murderer's identity. No arrest was ever made, however. An arrest proved unnecessary. The prime suspect was obviously a raving lunatic. She was committed to the asylum at Dewittville immediately after being questioned. Her subsequent suicide confirmed authorities in their belief of her guilt.

Her name was Fanny Premble. She was Ophelia that night. She was also Lucius Dascum's lover, or had been. The entire troupe was aware of their tumultuous relationship. She gave a brilliant performance. The Journal suggested that the depth of her distraction over the death of Polonius might have been an effect of premeditation. Various colleagues acknowledged that she had been in a highly agitated state. Lucius Dascum was preparing to quit the troupe and try his luck in New York. Apparently, he had refused to take her along. Watching the bedroom scene from the wings, she had fainted at the appearance of the ghost. When she awoke, the ghost was gone. Those attending had to remove her to the dressing rooms, for she threatened to disturb the action on stage. For a time it was doubtful she could play out Ophelia's madness and burial. Mr. Dascum was nowhere to be found. Mr. Keene arrived between scenes and managed to calm her. The audience gave her a standing ovation at curtain call and was doubly delighted when she affected continued lunacy.

She couldn't answer the investigators' questions. Doctor Rathbone was sent for and pronounced her unequivocally, perhaps irretrievably, mad. Such abrupt psychosis, the doctor said, was the effect of severe psychological trauma. Mr. Keene, who was present at the examination, described for the doctor Fanny Premble's reaction to the discovery of the body. According to Mr. Keene, the body was found shortly after the play ended, when the actors were leaving the theatre through the door to Potter's Alley. Fanny Premble, he said, approached the door with visible trepidation. He tried to spare her the gruesome sight, but she insisted on looking, and she looked long and hard. The face of the man was white. His stage robes were smeared with blood. His eyes were open. The dagger rose, emphatically, from deep in his chest. Mr. Keene said she stared for some moments. Then, she gasped. Before collapsing into his arms she muttered indistinctly. He wasn't absolutely sure of the words. "You're dead," he thought she said.

She stayed at the asylum for three months. All day long she picked wildflowers along the shore of the Lake and wove them into her hair. As she wandered the pretty banks she sang her lines from the play:

> He is dead and gone, lady,
> He is dead and gone:
> At his head a grass-green turf
> At his heels a stone.

Doctor Rathbone took an interest in her case. He accompanied her often on her walks. Sometimes, she spoke to him as if from a dream. One day he asked her, "Who, Fanny? Who is dead and gone?" She looked at him. For a moment her eyes seemed to clarify, then again she was remote. She answered in the same light tones with which she sang the song. "The one I killed, don't you know?"

"Lucius Dascum?"

> He is dead and gone, lady...
> He is dead and gone...

"Lucius Dascum?" Dr. Rathbone repeated.

"I saw him dead," she said. "I killed him." She paused, and her look was far away. "But he came back."

"What do you mean, Fanny?"

"To finish the play. He came back... He comes back."

On a fall evening she escaped the asylum. Her body was discovered the next morning floating in the shallows of the Lake. Wreaths of flowers tangled in her hair, and soft petals floated next to her.

*Spiritualism was a significant current in the culture
of America through the latter half of the nineteenth
century. The Spiritualists believed that an accessible spirit world existed alongside the material world
and that communication with the spirits of the
departed was possible. This was usually accom-
plished with the aid of a "medium", a man or
woman who had a facility in making spirit contact.
The Cassadaga Lake Free Association, which
became Lily Dale Assembly, had its origins in an
early group of Spiritualists from Laona. The Laona
Spiritualists, led by Mr. William Johnson, were
enthusiastic investigators into the phenomena of
spirit return. In the early days of Spiritualism they
often picnicked at a popular resort known as the
"Island" on Cassadaga Lake. Alva Lazell lost his
two daughters in the boating accident on which this
story is based. Grief and death were constants in
the lives of rural Victorians. Certainly, the success
of Spiritualism was in large part due to the measure
of comfort it offered to grieving survivors. The
meeting between Alva Lazell and William Johnson
occurred in my imagination.*

Alva Lazell

The matter of Alva Lazell and the spirit of Jarvis Wilcox thrilled the little group of Laona Spiritualists who were privy to it. The remarkable events occurred in the early days of Spiritualism when the truth of spirit return was only just being investigated. Jarvis Wilcox drowned in the waters of Cassadaga lake on a September afternoon in 1852. By then the Laona Spiritualists were true believers. For several years they had been communicating with the spirit world. The spirit world was becoming familiar to them in mysterious and exciting ways. Until Mr. William Johnson met Alva Lazell, however, no one had yet witnessed a material manifestation.

Seven young ladies died that afternoon with Jarvis Wilcox. They were part of a grand pleasure excursion to the Island. A day of fun and camaraderie had been planned. A party of forty young ladies and gentlemen had set out in three boats. Only one of the boats arrived safely at the Island. Jarvis' brother Martin explained afterwards what had happened. An oar lock in the little rowboat he had been pulling broke en route. He signalled Jarvis, who was following in the scow. Martin's boat began to take on water, and soon he and his passengers, the Misses Hoag and Abrams, Mr. Nichols and Mr. Goodrich, were in the lake. Seeing their companions thus, the young people on the scow, who were sitting on makeshift seats, impulsively leapt to their feet. The scow was a much larger craft carrying twenty persons. The effect of the sudden movement caused it to tilt. The young people reacted without thinking. They rushed across the deck in a vain attempt to right the scow. The scow rolled heavily. Every passenger, and Jarvis Wilcox, too, was thrown headlong through the rails and into the water.

The drownings plunged the town of Stockton into mourning. It was said the town would never be the same. Among the dead were Alva Lazell's two daughters, Lucy, age twenty-three, and Celia, eighteen. All of the young ladies were from the very best families. The entire town turned out for the funeral. The dead were buried in a common grave. A pretty monument was erected above them. Afterwards, the town carried on as best it could.

The loss of his daughters cast a cold and unrelenting gloom upon the soul of Alva Lazell. His days were bleak like an eternity of winter, and his nights were a torment of dream and nightmare. Alva was alone now, for his wife had died three years previously. Three years more had passed since the deaths of his daughters. The time had not mitigated his grief. Nor would it ever, Alva felt. Sometimes, half waking in the darkness, his daughters appeared before him. They seemed to float on the air, smiling, the way he remembered them. But always he awoke with a start to the hollow ache of their absence and the memory of their lifeless bodies sprawled wet on the wet lake bank.

In his distraction he wandered the lake shore where they had drowned. He stood upon the bank where they had lain, soaked through and lifeless. The lake was beautiful. The near shore was covered with floating lilies. The water was pure–Alva was glad of that. For his daughters had stayed in the water all night long. They had never been found until morning. The Island seemed close. So close, Alva thought, they ought to have been able to reach it. The Island lay upon the water so close, and beautiful, and serene as Death.

He never blamed Jarvis Wilcox. Jarvis Wilcox was a fine man, Alva knew that. He had known Jarvis Wilcox slightly before the accident. More than anything, he pitied the poor man. Martin Wilcox had managed to rescue the four from his sunken rowboat. But what could Jarvis have done? Twenty young bodies thrashed and churned the waters about him. The scow was out of reach. What would he, Alva, have done? Miss Hoag told Alva that Jarvis had retrieved the floating bench for her without which she never would have made the shore. Miss Hoag, watching from the bank with the hysterical company who had managed to reach safety, said Jarvis Wilcox was the last to go down. He must have worked to the limit of his endurance. He must have known he was about to die.

Jarvis Wilcox entered his dream. Beyond the smiling, disembodied faces of his daughters, Jarvis Wilcox rose up. His image was fearful. The set of his lips bespoke grim determination. But his eyes betrayed utter helplessness. Half waking, Alva could see the three faces in the darkness before him. Lucy and Celia lost burdened his soul, but even in his despair his grieving heart reached out to Jarvis Wilcox.

His neighbors in Stockton, mourners themselves, tried to comfort him. He told Dr. Harrison about his dream. Dr. Harrison had lost a daughter himself, Mary Augusta, his youngest, age fourteen. Dr. Harrison told Alva he must put off his grief. He would go mad.

Perhaps he was mad?

He had a vision. Standing on the lake shore, he imagined figures thrashing the clear water. The water churned white. The figures cried out although he heard no sound. Searching, he found Celia. He saw her panicked face across the water and her desperate struggle. Her heavy skirts were taking her down. And there was Lucy, reaching for her sister! For a long time his two daughters seemed to hold to one another. Around them the others cried out silently in panic and despair. Then, one by one, the figures began to disappear. Alva stared

35

as if in a trance. Soon, only his daughters were left. He almost cried out to them when they, too, dropped beneath the surface. When they were gone, the lake was still once more. But no. There was movement yet. A solitary figure, a man, was swimming, uncertainly, over the water where the seven were lost. Alva could see that he was searching. Alva recognized him immediately. It was Jarvis Wilcox.

Then, all was as it had been. The beauty of the lake returned. Soft ripples curled in the clear water beyond the lilies. And Alva returned to himself.

About the time of the drownings Mr. William Johnson had been a witness, in Laona, to the remarkable healing of Mr. Jeremiah Carter. In fact, he had been instrumental in precipitating that healing. Mr. Carter had for some time been in a debilitated state. Dr. Harrison had done all he could for him. Mr. Johnson, following his investigations into the spirit world, suggested they attempt spirit contact. Almost immediately Mr. Carter proved an extraordinary medium. The spirit of a certain Dr. Hedges, late of Chautauqua County, seemed eager to communicate with him. As he developed, Mr. Carter made a complete recovery. Now, under the guidance of Dr. Hedges, he himself had been healing the sick. Meanwhile, other mediums were emerging from the vicinity of Laona. The spirit world was revealing itself in all its beauty and possibility. Then it was, the Laona Spiritualists began to picnic on the Island. The Island's beauty and serenity they thought appropriate to spirit contact.

Alva knew nothing of the Spiritualists. Until he met Mr. Johnson he was unaware of their existence. Afterwards, after the two had become intimately acquainted, Mr. Johnson always spoke of their meeting as inevitable. Their meeting changed Alva Lazell's life.

They met on a September afternoon much like the afternoon of the drownings. The sun was low in the sky intermingling shadow and colored light on the lilies. The day had been warm. Mr. Johnson was in the habit, on his excursions to the Island, of leaving it at dusk to walk around the lake. He was a robust man and fond of physical exercise. As he walked that day he noticed from a considerable distance away a solitary figure gazing out upon the water. The man's introspection touched him. The man's concentration was intense. Alva was unaware of Mr. Johnson's approach. So preoccupied was he that Mr. Johnson remembered afterwards having feared intruding upon Alva's thoughts. When he was within several paces of the brooding man and Alva still had not noticed him, Mr. Johnson stopped. Never before had Mr. Johnson encountered an intensity of thought so profound. Alva's lips were trembling. Mr. Johnson turned in the direction of Alva's gaze over the water. There, beyond the lilies, he saw a man swimming. The man was obviously exhausted and in danger of going under. Mr. Johnson cried out to him. The cry startled Alva out of his reverie. He turned toward Mr. Johnson in surprise and confusion. Meanwhile, Mr. Johnson had removed his boots and trousers. Before Alva could speak, he dived in among the lilies and began to swim with strong strokes toward what Alva knew he would not find.

That was the last time Alva saw Jarvis Wilcox on the lake. Recollecting the occasion years afterwards, he often said he wished Jarvis would appear to him again. It took some time before Alva could make Mr. Johnson understand exactly what it was he had seen. Alva himself was incredulous. All along he had believed the swimming man to be an apparition, a product of his melancholy, visi-

ble only to himself. Mr. Johnson, of course, had lost
sight of Jarvis Wilcox on the water. He spent a great
deal of time searching beneath the surface until he finally
gave up and returned to shore. There Alva told him the
man he had tried to save from drowning had died three
years previously.

The profound significance of what had passed
between them affected both men to the very depths of
their being. For some time the two stood silent upon the
lake shore wondering what it all meant. Then, Alva
spoke. Alva, who for three years had avoided human
contact, who for three years had carried with him the
weight of a relentless and all consuming grief, there and
then on the lake shore opened his heart and soul to a
man he had never seen thirty minutes before. Mr.
Johnson listened.

Mr. Johnson well remembered the drownings. He
told Alva that he and his friends spoke often about them
and firmly believed that the spirits of the dead lingered
about the lake. He introduced Alva among the
Spiritualists. In the company of Mr. Carter Alva wandered the lake shore. He told Mr. Carter of his dream.
The Laona Spiritualists marveled. One day, on the
Island, Mr. Carter spoke in a trance. Lucy and Celia
Lavell, apparently, wished to leave their father a message.
Apparently, they had been trying for a long time without
success to contact him. Dr. Hedges, who had great experience in these matters, finally came to their aid. Dr.
Hedges showed them how to speak through Jeremiah
Carter. They wished Alva to know that they were in a
beautiful place. They wished him to know that they were
happy. They wished he would no longer grieve. One
day they would be together again. Until then they would
visit him in his dream. Jarvis Wilcox was with them.
Alva should hold his memory dear, for he was a fine and

a good spirit. Jarvis Wilcox had helped them all along. Jarvix Wilcox was responsible for Alva's meeting Mr. Johnson.

The message affected Alva Lazell deeply. His gloom left almost immediately. Nightly, his daughters appeared to him in his dream, smiling, the way he remembered them. No longer did he wake to the pain of his loneliness. Jarvis Wilcox left the dream. Alva remained an intimate companion to the Laona Spiritualists for the rest of his life. Shortly after his daughters' spirit message he visited Dr. Harrison. Dr. Harrison remarked on his greatly improved condition. During the course of their conversation Dr. Harrison told Alva that he, too, dreamed of his dead daughter. Curiously, Jarvis Wilcox had just entered his dream.

Silas H. Merrill was a well known inventor and well to do farmer of this town, and at the time of his death at Ashtabula was acting as a traveling agent for a mowing machine.

Last September the barn, shed, and horse barn on his old homestead, all well filled with newly gathered crops, were burned. The place at the time of the fire was occupied by a son-in-law of Mr. Merrill named M. J. Rhodes. Some time after the fire Mr. Rhodes, to the surprise of his neighbors, rented and moved into another house. The old homestead was then rented to a widow woman with one son. She stayed there only a few weeks and leaving, the place was rented to a family named Lawson who still occupy it. The numerous changes excited remark and surprise, and finally it leaked out that the old place was haunted by the spirit of the Ashtabula victim.

The above report under the title "Dayton's Ghost" appeared in the Jamestown Journal for January 23, 1878. The story was updated in the newspaper about a week later to an inconclusive end.

Dayton's Ghost

The old Merrill homestead on the Buffalo Road outside of Dayton was for many years after the unfortunate
death of Silas Merrill the subject of much interest and not
a little speculation among the citizens of that village.
That the house had indeed been haunted by the spirit of
Silas Merrill, a notion so thoroughly ridiculed at first, in
time was accepted with unabashed enthusiasm and a
degree of civic pride by growing numbers of Daytonians.
The house burned to the ground at the height of its noto-
riety, and the "ghost", apparently, disappeared. The citizenry, however, kept its memory alive through years of
prolonged and vehement debate. To be sure, the discus-
sion was often of a bemused nature, especially among
those who remembered Silas Merrill. Ghost or not,
everyone agreed from the very beginning that such a man
was eminently capable of returning from the dead.

Much was made of the fact that three families, includ-
ing that of Mr. Merrill's only daughter, occupied and
abandoned the house in quick succession after his death.
The village had already registered surprise, before any
mention of the ghost was made, when Dorothy Merrill
and her husband, Mr. Matthew Rhodes, after assuming
ownership, removed so quickly to a rented house in town.
The talk began in earnest when the widow Bailey and her
son followed suit. Whereupon, Mrs. Annie Lawson,
whose family was the last and longest to occupy the
house, opened the floodgates of speculation by an imme-
diate and vociferous insistence on the presence of the
ghost. She maintained that the house echoed each night
with loud, inexplicable sounds and that in the morning
she invariably found her furniture displaced, scratched or
even overturned. Folks said that sounded a lot like Silas
Merrill.

Doubters suggested that Mrs. Lawson was enjoying the new found celebrity status that talk of the ghost gave to her. However that may be, the curious, who began to stroll out to the farm, seemed to corroborate her testimony by reports of unusual soundings emanating from the house. The village eventually felt it necessary to dispatch two of its finest to investigate the premises.

The report of the Messrs. Barnhardt and Bartlett was inconclusive. Although they found no physical evidence of a ghost, beyond certain scrapings on Annie Lawson's dining room suite, they could not help but be affected by the grim state of panic in which they discovered the Lawson children. Eddie, who was eight, claimed to have actually seen the ghost. He described it as a "tramp", which sounded to many much like Silas Merrill, and said he had awakened several nights past to find it looking in on him through the bedroom window. Since then, the children had been sleeping downstairs near their parents. Mr. Lawson was suspiciously noncommittal about the affair. Mr. Bartlett at one point thought he heard foot-steps behind him on the stairs. Mr. Barnhardt attributed that to the hordes of rats and mice that infested the house.

The ghost, it was determined, whatever it was, was not malevolent. As the days passed its reputation grew. Annie Lawson kept the village informed of its activity. The Lawson family persevered in the house for almost six months. Finally, they, too, had enough. By the time they moved out Annie Lawson had achieved a good deal of respect for her pluck. She told everyone it wasn't fear– even the children had ceased to fear the ghost–it was the "damned inconvenience". As for any doubt that may initially have been raised concerning the ghost's identity, that had long since been dispelled when the ghost proved every bit as single minded, careless, and inconsiderate as

Silas had been. The only question that remained was why it should have returned at all. The presence of the vermin was sufficient answer to that.

Silas Merrill died in the town of Ashtabula in the summer of 1877. He had traveled to Ohio to demonstrate the improved Rat Catcher he hoped to patent. Although he owned a substantial farm, Silas' heart really wasn't in it. Silas Merrill fancied himself an inventor. The homestead in Dayton contained two barns, one for the horses, the other for the workings of Silas' imagination in various stages of development. Folks encouraged him. Most of his creations, however, never caught on. He did have some success among his neighbors with a Perpetual Motion Scarecrow; and his Perfumed Bee Smoker, a curiosity afterwards displayed with pride by those who owned one, had actually attracted the attention of a manufacturer in the East. But his inventions never seemed to carry beyond the beauty of their conception.

That didn't stop Silas. "Perseverance is the key," he told his poor wife Helen over and over again, driving her to distraction, and, some said, to an early grave herself. Helen told Silas he was an obstinate old fool. Perseverance had already scarred his body. Perseverance was likely to be the end of him. Was, as it turned out. He walked with a limp and a cane, the result of a fall from a barn roof at a raising to which he had supplied the liquor. He made the best corn liquor in the county. Folks respected him for that. He made it on a still of his own design and construction. A man so naturally clumsy, however, should never have fooled with drink.

The Rat Catcher showed promise. Of late years Silas had been waging a ruthless campaign against the rats and mice that plagued his barns and shed. The intensity with which he pursued them had become an obsession and a matter of talk among his neighbors. He had fashioned all manner of elegant devices for their capture. He had experimented with endless strange and exotic baits. His intricate wire and spring affairs, however, though marvelous to look at, yielded only the occasional rat; and these, it seemed, were of the fat and lazy end of the species. The Improved Rat Catcher, on the other hand, immediately and consistently proved capable of large scale extermination. Brilliant in its simplicity, it was not only efficient, it was easily manufactured. A simple wooden barrel filled three quarters with water, upon which barley or oats might be floated —that was all there was to it. The rats and mice in endeavoring to secure the grain fell into the barrel and drowned. Silas dreamed it up one rainy night while unable to sleep. He tried it that very night in the shed and was rewarded in the morning with thirty-six drowned rats. Over the course of months of experimentation, in which time he kept careful records, the results were truly impressive. In eight months he calculated to have killed some one thousand, two hundred and seventeen of the pernicious species. The examination of his traps every morning became a source of pride and pleasure for him. For the trip to Ashtabula he painted his barrels with suitable testimonials to their efficiency and, as an afterthought, fixed a series of downturned metal spikes on their inside rims to keep the rats from jumping out.

On the afternoon of his arrival in Ashtabula he parked his wagon on Main Street and began to challenge a bewildered audience to try the Rat Catcher overnight. Before he was well along in his exhortations the horse shied and threw him out on his head.

"Drunk, probably," said Dorothy Merrill. She dutifully returned the corpse to Dayton and buried it in the family plot at the farm. Three days later, already installed in the house with her husband, the shed and both barns, all well filled with newly gathered crops, burned to the ground. All that remained after the fire burned out was the blackened ruins of the still and two intact Rat Catchers filled with fresh water and drowned rats.

Dorothy Merrill never explained to anyone's satisfaction why she left the house so hurriedly after the fire. Annie Lawson never had any doubt as to the reason. For years afterward Annie Lawson insisted she could have lived with the ghost if it hadn't been for the dead rats that kept showing up around the house. The true believers were convinced that Silas, or his ghost, was through some carelessness responsible for the fires that destroyed the shed and barns and eventually the house itself. In the days that followed the house fire most Daytonians rode out to look at the smoldering ruins. Those who looked carefully discovered amid the debris what looked like the remains of several Improved Rat Catchers.

The Panama Conglomerate is reputed to be the largest outcrop of ocean quartz in the world. The rock originated as sediment deposited by a Paleozoic river. Three hundred million years ago that river flowed into an inland sea. Millions of tons of particles over millions of years compacted to form the Panama Rocks. Violent geological activity raised them to their present elevation, and retreating glaciers carved the labyrinthine passages among them. The rocks tower amid an old world forest of hardwood and evergreen. The area has never been logged.

There is a mystical quality about this imposing landscape. Certainly, the rocks merit their considerable local reputation. Legend holds that treasure is buried among their passageways. "Panama Rocks" draws not so much on local legend as it does on the physical power of the rocks as a backdrop to the spiritual power of mother love.

Panama Rocks

Mr. Harold Augustus Robinson, philanthropist and beloved citizen of Jamestown, died peacefully of natural causes at his home on Lakeview Avenue September 15, 1959. His secretary and lifelong companion, Mrs. Mary Osborne, was at his side. Mr. Robinson left no heir. The bulk of his considerable estate he divided between the Gustavus Adolphus Orphanage and the Randolph Children's Home. Among his effects the following letter appeared:

February 22, 1889

Dearest Harry,

On this your second birthday I take pen in hand to record for you my feelings and my love. In a little while I shall be no more and you will be alone. The thought fills my soul with dread. As I look upon you, for know you are lying this moment in my lap, sleeping the sleep of the innocent, I am struck by your beauty which is not of this earth. How can it be that you are flesh of my flesh? Your hands are clasped one upon the other, and you breathe in almost perfect silence. What callouses await those hands when my flesh is gone and you are alone? What hard, rattling breath? You will never know your mother's love. This night you will never know. Know then, that I take this night with me to the grave, and I take your beauty, too, leaving behind my love. Know, dear Harry, that if ever beyond the grave a breath of something more remains, my breath it will be. My breath of mother's love. I kiss you, my darling, now and forever. Goodbye.

Mother

Harold Augustus Robinson, age seven, motherless, loved more than anything else to spend the day playing with his friend Mary among the Rocks. The Rocks were fantastic. They were enormous, majestic things, suitable dwellings for the giants and ogres Mary told him about. They looked to Harold like medieval castles, towering and impregnable. Narrow passages ran among them in many directions so that one might hide and never be found. Mary told Harold that somewhere in these passages robbers' treasure was buried. Silver coins and gold, stolen by two mad Frenchmen when this was a new world and the French were exploring. The robbers were caught and hanged, but the treasure was never found.

Mary and the Rocks were the best part of Harold's life. Harold was a sensitive and lonely child. He lived with his grandmother, a woman named Catherine Walker to whom Mary was companion and housekeeper. The house they lived in was the best in Panama. It had white columns on the front and a porch upstairs. It was built by Harold's grandfather, whom Harold knew from the photograph hanging in the parlor. Harold's mother died of consumption when he was two years old. His father ran off West to mine silver. His father paid dutifully for Harold's keep even though Mr. Walker told him that wouldn't be necessary. Mr. Walker was dead now, too. Harold was expected to be quiet in the house.

The Rocks were only a short distance away, across two dirt roads and a creek known as the Little Brokenstraw. They were on land owned by Mr. Arthur Davis. That they were so close was fortunate, because Harold's grandmother frequently wanted him out of the house. Every time Mr. Henry came to call, Mrs. Walker had Mary take Harold to the Rocks. Mr. Henry had been calling for as long as Harold could remember. Most of the time he had sent messages to Harold's grandmother before he came. The day before his visits Mary spent in a frenzy of housework. More and more, however, Mr. Henry had been appearing unannounced. The first time this happened, seeing the buggy approach from the parlor window, Mrs. Walker went into a panic. She ordered Mary to take Harold out of the house immediately, then ran upstairs to prepare herself. After that, Harold noticed, she seemed constantly to be looking out the window. Mr. Henry was a lawyer. He had black hair and a mustache. He drove the buggy fast, and once, when he passed Harold and Mary on the road, Harold saw him drinking from a flask.

"Why does Grandmother chase us out of the house when Mr. Henry comes?" Harold asked Mary one day. They were sitting on the trail above the Rocks eating sandwiches out of a picnic basket.

Mary thought a moment. "Mr. Henry is your grandmother's gentleman friend."

"Does Grandmother like for him to come?" A breeze blew up among the trees and Harold looked into their branches to watch until the leaves stopped rustling. Mary poured two glasses of lemonade. She handed one of them to Harold. Then she looked at him with a serious look. "I think she does. Mr. Henry is very handsome."

"He thinks you're pretty." The fact had not escaped her. Mr. Henry often spoke to her. Sometimes, when he came unexpectedly, Mrs. Walker kept him waiting. He waited in the kitchen, and if Harold and Mary were not yet gone, he asked her questions that made her blush. He referred to Harold as the "young man". This morning, as they went out the door, leaving him alone, he remarked in a suggestive way that perhaps one day he would go with them to the Rocks and Mary would have two young men.

"Well, I thank him for thinking so."

"I don't think Grandmother likes him," Harold said. He pulled a few crumbs from the crust of his bread and tried to feed them to a beetle that was crawling in the grass next to his hand.

"Oh, but she must," Mary said. "Why else would she let him come?"

The beetle wasn't interested. It changed direction and moved off at a faster pace. "Maybe she' s mad."

Mary smiled. "Nonsense," she said. "What do you know about mad?"

"Like the two Frenchmen," said Harold. He placed the rest of the sandwich into his mouth. "I think she must be mad."

Mrs. Walker was upset. Mr. Henry had not shown up for more than two weeks nor sent any word. It had been raining steadily, and Harold and Mary had had to stay in the house. Mrs. Walker's agitation grew with each passing day. She was constantly irritable. She found all sorts of things for Mary to do. Harold stayed well out of her way. Finally, Mrs. Walker retired to her bedroom. All day long she called to Mary from the top of the stairs to bring her this or that, food or medicine. When Mr. Henry arrived one morning, unexpectedly, she was still in bed. She told Mary to take Harold to the Rocks and not to return until supper time.

Waiting in the kitchen, Mr. Henry seemed not at all impatient. While Mary sliced bread into the picnic basket, he stood with his hands in his pockets, watching. Harold was out in the yard. The rain had stopped, but the air was still heavy and the day cloudy. Mr. Henry leaned against the table.

"You're out to the Rocks again, eh?"

Mary nodded.

"It'll be warm today," said Mr. Henry. He had a fresh haircut, slicked back, and his mustache was trimmed. "Cool between them Rocks, I'll bet." He straightened up. "Nice spot for a rendez-vous. You know what that means, a rendez-vous?"

Mary didn't answer. She continued packing the picnic basket, avoiding Mr. Henry's eyes.

"Sure. You know what that means. Pretty girl like you." He began to pace around the kitchen. When he came to the window, he stopped to look out into the yard. For some minutes he stood there watching. Then, without turning around, he spoke. "'Well now. Look at this. The young man talks to himself." The spectacle seemed to amuse him. He watched a bit longer, his hands still in his pockets and his back to Mary. "Sure does," he chuckled. "Talks to himself."

"He's talking to the wind," Mary said.

"Is he now?" Mr. Henry turned around and faced her. "Talking to the wind? What's he saying?"

"I don't know."

Mr. Henry looked out the window again. The wind was blowing, gently. Harold's face was raised at an angle as if to catch the breeze. When Mary rose from her chair, Mr. Henry faced around. Mary picked up the picnic basket and walked to the door. As she opened it, Mr. Henry smiled. "Curious boy, that." he said.

The buggy was still parked in the side yard when they returned. Mr. Henry was sitting on the back porch in front of a small table, playing at solitaire. He was smoking a cigar. The day had been warm, and he had removed his jacket. "I'm invited to dinner," he told them by way of greeting. He took a long pull on his cigar and blew out the smoke in a steady gray stream. From inside

the house Mrs. Walker called to Mary. Harold watched
the smoke linger and spread in the still air. "Nothing like
a good cigar, young man," Mr. Henry said. He held up
the cigar so that Harold could see it. "Makes you feel
like king of the world. Keeps the flies off, too." He
winked.

"They smell bad," Harold said.

"Oh?" Mr. Henry looked at him more closely.
"Depends on who's smelling 'em." He rolled the cigar
between his fingers. Presently, he smiled. "Maybe you'd
like to try it?"

Harold shook his head. The air stirred, breaking
apart the gray smoke. The sound of cabinets opening
and the clatter of pots issued from the kitchen. Mr.
Henry's horse, grazing on the grass in the yard next to
the buggy, whinnied. Mr. Henry clamped down on the
cigar between his teeth. A bit of ash fell into his lap, and
he brushed it away with the back of his hand. He began
to turn the cards, slowly and methodically. Harold
watched. Out of the unencumbered corner of his mouth
Mr. Henry asked, "What do you do at them Rocks all
day?"

"Play," said Harold.

There was nothing left of the cigar now but a little
stub. Mr. Henry took it out of his mouth and examined
it. He drew on it one more time, then threw the butt
into the yard. "Play?" he said.

"Sometimes we look for treasure."

Again, Mr. Henry looked at Harold close. The child
was thin and frail. Mr. Henry suddenly coughed deep in
his throat. Turning in his chair, he leaned over the railing
and spat into the yard. He pulled a handkerchief from
his pocket and wiped his mouth. Then he looked at
Harold a long time. "Treasure, eh? There's no pirates
around here."

"Robbers," said Harold.

Mr. Henry turned a card. "All right," he said. He thought a moment. Once again he looked at Harold, as if what he was about to say was serious and confidential. "Tell you what. Between you and me, if there's any treasure around here, it's right there in that house."

A sudden gust of wind blew up scattering the cards across the porch floor and into the yard. Mr. Henry cursed. Mary appeared at the door and came out onto the porch. Mrs. Walker was sending her to town for coffee. She took Harold by the hand and led him off. Standing now, retrieving the cards, Mr. Henry called after them, "You keep your eyes open, young man."

The weather turned hot. The woods began to dry up. Harold and Mary played at the Rocks nearly every day. Mrs. Walker kept the house closed up and the shades drawn to preserve the coolness. Mr. Henry paid more or less regular visits. He often remained now after Harold and Mary returned from the Rocks, and sometimes he stayed well into the evening. He began to pay more attention to Harold, watching him play in the yard and speaking to him especially if no one else was around. One day he took Harold for a ride in the buggy. Harold's grandfather was a rich man, he told him. Did he know that? He drank from the flask while he was driving.

When they returned, it was nearly dark. Mary was waiting on the porch. Mr. Henry went inside to say goodnight to Mrs. Walker. Mary said Harold could play in the yard a while longer. When Mr. Henry came out, Harold was standing near the edge of the woods. The sun had gone down and the light was dim. The wind was blowing through the leaves in the trees. Mr. Henry stopped in the shadow of the house. For several minutes he did not move. Harold was looking intently into the trees. Clearly, the boy was speaking, but Mr. Henry could not hear what he said. Mr. Henry moved a little closer through the shadows. Silently, he stepped into the woods. The leaves rustled overhead. He stood perfectly still and listened. Suddenly, the wind gusted. Branches swayed and the leaves turned so that their silver undersides shone in the early moonlight. Harold faced around and saw Mr. Henry standing there.

Mr. Henry stepped out of the woods. He looked upon Harold for a moment, then up into the trees. Neither of them spoke. Finally, Mr. Henry broke the silence. "You'd better get inside. There's liable to be a storm tonight."

Three days later Mrs. Walker received a letter from Mr. Henry saying that he was leaving town for an indefinite stay and that he would call when he returned. There had been no rain. The Little Brokenstraw was nothing but a trickle. At the Rocks Harold asked Mary about his grandfather. Mary told him his grandfather had been a successful businessman and a teacher. As a young man he had invested in oil in Pennsylvania and made a fortune. He taught at the Normal School in Fredonia, and for many years he was a member of the state assembly. He died six months after Harold's mother. Mary remembered Mr. Walker fondly. She promised to take Harold to see his marker in the cemetery.

"Mr. Henry says there's treasure in the house."

Mary frowned. "Don't you listen to Mr. Henry."

Augustus John Walker
Born July 23, 1833
Died September 18, 1890
The Lord Giveth, and the Lord Taketh Away

A squarish, respectable stone, not overly large. Made of granite. "He was always kind to me," Mary said. She was holding Harold's hand. August John Walker's accomplishments were engraved on the back side of the marker: Captain, 112th NY Volunteers; Board of Directors, Northern Pa. Oil and Gas Co.; Professor of Mathematics, Normal School at Fredonia; New York State Assembly, 1868-1874, 1878-1882; Philanthropist; Friend to Chautauqua County. "His friends called him Gus."

"That's my name," said Harold.

"Yes," said Mary.

"His birthday's next week," Harold said.

"That's right." Mary squeezed his hand for having read the marker correctly. She had taught him to read. "How old would he be?"

Harold counted on his fingers. After some hesitation he came up with the answer. "Sixty-one."

"He wasn't an old man at all." Mary smiled. "There was an accident. He fell off the roof of your house. Everybody came to the funeral. You were there."

"With my mother?"

"No. She was already dead. Your father was there, though. So was I. You were with me."

Mrs. Walker had not wanted them to go to the cemetery. She never went there herself. She had not made an issue of it, however. She told Mary to stop at the post office on the way back. When they returned in the early afternoon, she was sitting in the darkened parlor sipping from a tall glass. A fly buzzed noisily at the window inside the shade. There had been no letters. Mrs. Walker was wearing a dark summer house dress that hung loosely on her frame. Since the death of her husband, she had lost considerable weight, and the doctor had told her she must eat better. Her hair was brushed. It was chestnut colored, hardly gray, and it hung to the middle of her back. Despite the thinness she was still a handsome woman.

"Will you have some lunch?" Mary asked her.

The fly kept buzzing back and forth battering against the shade and the window pane. Mrs. Walker closed her eyes as though the sound were beating inside her head. "Can't you kill it?" she said. "What's the boy doing?"

"He's in the kitchen," Mary answered. Mrs. Walker shook her head. Out of the photograph on the wall behind her Augustus John Walker looked over her shoulder.

"Why was Gus on the roof?" Harold asked. They were standing in the yard looking up toward the second story porch.

"He was replacing some shingles."

"Where?"

Mary pointed. The roof sloped gently where Augustus John Walker had been standing. It was at a point to the right of the porch. The porch had low railings. Harold had never been on the porch. In fact, he had never seen anyone on it. The porch was attached to Mrs. Walker's bedroom. Harold followed a line to the ground below and the flagstones where Augustus John Walker must have landed.

"Did you see him fall?"

"No," said Mary. "Your grandmother did, I think. I remember she was on the porch with him. She sent me for Mr. Davis. I was with you."

"Do you remember my mother?"

Mary looked down upon him. She took his hand. "Come," she said. "Let's sit in the shade."

They walked to the edge of the woods and sat down in the grass near the path to the Rocks. The grass had turned brown. In the trees the cicadas began to sing. The leaves stirred.

"I like the wind," said Harold.

"I know you do." Mary took his hand and held it on her knee. "Your mother was beautiful. I only saw her a few times. The last time was just before she died. You lived in Jamestown then. She came to talk to your grandfather. She was very sick." She looked into Harold's eyes. "You look like your mother."

"Where's my father?"

"I'm not sure. California, I think."

The cicadas stopped singing. A whisper of breeze caressed Harold's hair. "Listen," said Mary. "I'm going to tell you something you don't know. I'm an orphan, too. My mother and father are dead. That's why I live with you. Your grandfather brought me here after my mother died. We're both orphans."

They were silent for a moment. From out of the woods, unseen, a bird sang three notes. Ever so slightly the breeze picked up and brushed the side of Mary's face, then all was still again. Mary smiled. "Your grandfather..."

"Call him Gus."

"We came on the train. From Albany. That's where I lived. It's way on the other side of the state." She paused while the bird repeated its song. "He was my mother's friend."

Harold drew his hand away. "Was my mother in Albany?"

"No," said Mary. "I don't think so. I never saw her. Of course, I was only a young girl. I only saw your grandfather...Gus... I only saw Gus when he came to our house."

The child reflected on these things. No one had ever told him about the accident. He couldn't really remember his grandfather or his mother, but this knowledge of the past seemed to connect him to them. While he was thinking, Mrs. Walker called to Mary from the porch. Mary excused herself and went up to the house. Harold lay down and looked into the trees.

That night, after Mrs. Walker retired to her room, Harold and Mary went into the parlor to look at the photograph. Mary said she saw a resemblance between Harold and Augustus John. Harold stared at the picture a long time. He thought Gus looked awfully like Mary.

"You're filling his head with ideas," Mrs. Walker said. "I don't like it. He's always mooning around." The interest Harold took in her husband upset Mrs. Walker. More than once she had seen Harold gazing at the roof from which Augustus John had fallen. Now she heard him use the familiar nickname in speaking to Mary. The sound of her husband's name coming from the boy irritated her. She told Mary to stop telling him stories.

Two weeks had passed. Still, there was no word from Mr. Henry. Mrs. Walker sent Mary to the post office every day. There had been a single slight rain, but the sun had come out hot afterwards and all was as dry as ever. No one in town could remember such a drought. Finally, a letter arrived. Mr. Henry had returned. He wrote that he would call on the following Tuesday. Mrs. Walker planned an extravagant meal for him. Harold and Mary were to go to the Rocks in the morning and return by noon so that Mary could prepare it. On Monday evening Mrs. Walker set the dining room table herself using the fine china.

In the morning Harold and Mary were off before Mr. Henry showed up. At the edge of the Little Brokenstraw they met Mr. Davis looking into the dry creekbed. "Mornin' to you," he said when he saw them. "You're about early." Mr. Davis liked them both. He lived with his wife in the back rooms of the inn to accommodate visitors to the Rocks. Sometimes he invited them in to visit. "Never seen it so dry," he said. "Good mornin' to you, young man. Say, Lucy's got some fresh donuts at home." Mrs. Davis, as always, was pleased to see them. Since there were no guests, she had them sit in the dining room. "How's Catherine?" she asked, pouring coffee. "We never see her anymore."

"Thank you," said Mary. "She doesn't go out very much."

"I should have her to tea," said Mrs. Davis.

"That lawyer still comin' around?" said Mr. Davis. Mary nodded. "Mr. Henry. Yes."

Mr. Davis exchanged a glance with his wife. He had been great friends with Gus. They had fished together for many years on Mr. Davis' property and often at the lake. Mr. Davis had made all the arrangements after the accident.

"She's got to have friends," Mrs. Davis said. She cut a melon that Harold and Mary had brought in the picnic basket and placed a slice before Harold. Then she pushed the plate of donuts toward him. When he reached for one, she smiled. "You have your mother's eyes."

"Held him on my lap when he was six days old," Mr. Davis said, leaning toward Mary. "Now look at him. You found that treasure yet, son?"

Harold shook his head.

"Well, you keep lookin'."

Mrs. Davis put her hand on Mary's arm. "Now, Mary. I'm going to give you a peach pie for Catherine. You stop here on your way home and take it. We haven't had guests for three days."

"Did Gus like the Rocks?" The sound of Harold's

59

voice surprised them all. Usually, at the inn, he didn't speak. For a moment no one answered. Then, Mr. Davis' face relaxed with pleasure.

"Gus? Sure." He winked at Mary. "He loved 'em. All the time bringin' folks to see 'em. Big shots. He brought the old governor once."

"Your mother used to play there, too," said Mrs. Davis.

Mr. Davis chuckled. "The old governor had to climb up. Gus was scared to death he'd fall. Nearly did, halfway up. Kept tellin' Gus not to crowd him. You know how the wind blows up there. Gus couldn't hear him."

"Did it hurt when he fell?"

Mr. and Mrs. Davis both looked to Mary. Mr. Davis sighed. He shook his head before he answered. "I doubt he felt anything." He put his hand on Harold's shoulder. "He was a good man, your grandfather. Now, you listen here. You like fishin'? You come on over here any time and we'll go. Just you and me."

Mrs. Davis had them leave the picnic basket so as to be sure to return for the pie. At the Rocks Harold surveyed the possible ascents to determine which of them Gus had most probably tried with the old governor. Halfway up, preceding Mary, he stopped. The wind was blowing. "Can you hear me?" he asked. Mary said she could. When they reached the top, they sat down to rest. "Gus must have been deaf," said Harold.

He put his head back to catch the wind. Mary sprawled in the dry and brittle grass. "Listen," said Harold. The wind made the slightest sound.

"I don't hear anything," said Mary.

"Listen to the wind."

Mary closed her eyes. She was still breathing hard after the climb. The wind blew softly against her face.

"What do you hear?"

Harold didn't answer for a moment. "Nothing," he finally said. He lay down upon his back and looked up into the sky. "Not now."

"Sometimes?" Mary asked.

"Yes," said Harold.

"What?"

"Sometimes I hear my mother."

The pie was still warm when they picked it up. Back at the house the buggy was parked in the side yard and the horse unhitched. The house was quiet. Mrs. Walker and Mr. Henry were nowhere to be seen. Mary put the pie on the counter. She looked into the dining room. The table was set very prettily for two. She pulled a crystal vase from the china closet and returned with it to the kitchen. "Will you see if there are any roses?" she asked Harold.

As he passed, the horse looked at him. The roses were surviving quite well despite the heat and the shiny beetles on their petals. Harold walked around to the front of the house. He looked up at the porch. Mr. Henry stood there, staring down at him.

"What's the matter, young man? Ain't you glad to see me?" he turned to say something into the bedroom, then turned back chuckling. His right hand held the flask. "You come around to my carriage," he said. "I've got something for you."

Harold went into the kitchen where Mary was trimming the beef. He told her Mr. Henry was upstairs. And Grandmother, too. Presently, Mr. Henry appeared. "The young man ain't glad to see me," he said. He bowed, looking at Mary close. "Don't suppose you are?"

At the door he beckoned to Harold to follow. A small white box lay on the seat of the buggy. Mr. Henry picked it up and handed it to Harold. There was tissue paper inside. Harold unfolded the paper and pulled out a narrow brown object made of India rubber. It was a moment before he realized it was a toy cigar.

During the afternoon Mr. Henry slept in the guest bedroom, unused since the accident. Mrs. Walker called Mary into the parlor to talk. She wanted to know how Mary's father had died. Mary told her there had been a hunting accident. She didn't know many of the details. Her father had died before she was born.

"You never knew your father?" Mrs. Walker asked.

"No," said Mary.

"When did this happen?"

"In '69," said Mary. "In August. I was born the following March."

Mrs. Walker stared at her. The shades were still drawn, but the room was hot. The smell of roasting beef came from the kitchen. "He was in the Assembly?" Mrs. Walker asked.

"Yes," said Mary. "That's how he knew Mr. Walker."

Two tiny beads of perspiration appeared on Mrs. Walker's upper lip. "Do you know why my husband brought you here?" she asked.

"He did it out of kindness," Mary said after a moment. She looked into her lap. Never before had Mrs. Walker betrayed an interest in her past. "He was always kind to me. After my mother died, I had no one."

"Mr. Henry knew your father."

Mary felt a sudden chill. She raised her eyes to find Mrs. Walker still staring at her. The look on Mrs. Walker's face frightened her. Mrs. Walker waited until Mary regained her composure before continuing.

"You didn't know that? You never saw him in

62

Albany?" She could see that Mary hadn't. She paused. "He was your father's friend."

"I don't want to talk about it," said Mary.

"*Oh, but ain't it about time?*" The voice was calm and ingratiating. Both women started. Mr. Henry stepped into the doorway and bowed ceremoniously. His clothes were wrinkled and his hair uncombed. "May I join you, ladies?" Seated, he turned to Mary. "Nice fella, your father. You'd 'a been proud of him."

Mrs. Walker looked at him coldly. He smiled a grim smile at her. "You're a pig," she said.

"She ought to know," he said to Mary.

Mrs. Walker rose, intending to leave. Mr. Henry blocked her way. "Sit down," he said. "Pigs can't hurt you." She sat back in her chair and Mr. Henry turned once more to Mary. "Ain't she lovely," he said. "Wisht I could'a seen her twenty years ago." He leaned back, pointedly ignoring Mrs. Walker. "Doesn't know what she wants, though," he said. "Happens sometimes when they get old." He leaned again toward Mary. "She's telling the truth. Me and your daddy go back a long way."

"What do you want?" said Mary.

"Me? Nothing. Not any more. Don't know why I bothered in the first place. Pride, I suppose. What d'you say m'Lady. Never could measure up to that old man, could I?"

"Get out of my house."

"Now you hold on. I ain't done yet. Mary here wants to know about her pa. You know what he told me, Mary? Told me old Gus give him money. Couldn't say enough about old Gus, your pa. Not that he didn't know how to make a dollar hisself. Said all you got to do was hold out your hand and they give it to you. Your pa was always holdin' out his hand."

He coughed into his fist. When he lowered his hand,

a little dollop of phlegm remained on his mustache. Emphatically, he pulled the handkerchief from his pocket and rubbed it across his mouth. "'Scuse me," he said. He blew his nose. Still holding the handkerchief, he continued. "Bit of a stiff at poker, though. Old Gus bailed him out more'n once, I'd say. Couldn't hold his liquor neither. That's what killed him." He looked at Mrs. Walker. "Don't suppose old Gus minded, d'you, m'Lady?"

The question lingered in the oppressive air for some minutes. No one spoke. Mr. Henry squeezed the wadded handkerchief in his hand and watched the two women. He blew his nose again. Then he chuckled. "Old Gus got me out of there quick." He shook his head as if in admiration. "Can't say as I blame him." He looked at Mary. "Your ma was a looker, too." Again, he paused, folded the handkerchief and stuffed it into his pocket. Then he turned once more to Mrs. Walker. "Tell me, Catherine," he said, in a matter of fact way, "what'd you have done in his place?"

He stared at her a long time, as if really expecting an answer. Finally, she spoke. "Will you leave now?"

"Sure. Soon's I tell Mary what he did do. Kept right on. Give your ma everything she wanted. You, too. I used to see 'em together. You were with 'em sometimes. Pretty little family. Lady Jane over there never suspected nothin'. I'm the one figured it out. Only had to look at that picture."

Mrs. Walker stiffened. Mary looked up. The image of Augustus John Walker bearing a benign expression overlooked the room. Mr. Henry folded his hands and smiled his grim smile.

From beyond the drawn shade and the heat and silence of the room the sound of cicadas could be heard. Mr. Henry and the two women sat on, unspeaking, an interminable time, until at last Mr. Henry was satisfied. Once more he leaned toward Mary. He looked at her close before he spoke, and when he spoke, it was in a confidential way but loud enough so that Mrs. Walker could hear. "I'll tell you another thing," he said, motioning at Mrs. Walker, "She knew what was going on. I sent her a letter."

Mrs. Walker closed her eyes. Mr. Henry leaned back and crossed his legs. He looked to Mrs. Walker, then back to Mary. "You know what else I did? I come out here. After old Gus run me off. I come out here to watch. I been here since before your ma died. I been watchin'."

"Don't," Mrs. Walker whispered.

"I was here the day you come." He lowered his voice. "I was here the day Gus fell."

Abruptly, the cicadas stopped buzzing. Even in the oppressive heat Mary felt cold. Finally, Mr. Henry stood up. Taking out his handkerchief, he wiped his brow. He stood in the doorway for several minutes looking over the two women. Then, he smiled. "Sorry I can't stay to dinner," he said. "Don't get up, ladies. I'll see my own way out." Still he didn't move. He lingered a moment longer, looking hard at the photograph on the wall. Then he looked at Mary and bowed. "Ask her what really happened on that roof," he said. And he was out of the room.

Harold was playing by the side of the road when the buggy approached. He turned at its sound and watched it come on. Mr. Henry was looking at him. When the buggy got close, Harold stepped away from the roadbed and stood motionless. Mr. Henry drew alongside and stopped.

"How about a ride?" Mr. Henry said.

Harold didn't move.

"Come on. We got time."

As soon as Harold stepped into the buggy the wind started up. Harold looked around quickly. Mr. Henry whipped the horse without warning, throwing the child off balance. Grasping Harold by the arm, he pulled him onto the seat. "I get tired in that house all day," he said. "Don't know how your grandmother stands it."

The road curved out of sight of the house. Mr. Henry loosened the reins, and the horse trotted on with a rhythmic clattering. "Say," said Mr. Henry. "I've got an idea. Whyn't you show me those Rocks?"

Tiny pebbles kicked up from the horse's hooves clicked off the undercarriage. They drove to the upper road so that Mr. Henry would not have to climb. Mr. Henry parked the buggy in a clearing among the trees. The sun was low in the sky and there was not a sound of bird or insect. The wind blew steadily, now. As he led Mr. Henry along the narrow path into the woods, Harold listened.

"Might get some rain finally," said Mr. Henry.

The path rose slightly. Ahead of them on the right, where the Rocks began, the trees gave off and the sunlight was brighter. Harold reached this spot well ahead of Mr. Henry. When Mr. Henry caught up to him, he was standing on the tallest peak. Clumps of dried grass grew out of the stone and a forest of desiccated, rotting trees. The wind blew stronger here. Mr. Henry was breathing rapidly. He looked out over the splendor of the Rocks to where they crashed on the forest floor. "Long way down," he said. Then, wiping his forehead, "That's a hot wind."

"It's usually windy up here," Harold said.

Mr. Henry pulled a cigar from his jacket pocket and wet the tip with his tongue. Seeing that Harold was watching, he bit down on it with his teeth, then he reached into his pocket for another. This he held out to Harold in silent offering. Harold shook his head. "Hope I can get the damn thing lit," Mr. Henry said. He sat down on the rock, in the coarse brown grass that grew upon it. "Come on over here and shield that wind, would you?"

The cigar lit on the third match. Mr. Henry pulled on it hard until a red ash appeared at the tip. The smoke he blew out dissipated quickly in the wind. "Thank you," he said.

He tried to blow a smoke ring, but the wind was too strong. For a few moments he smoked on in silence. Then he looked over at Harold who was sitting a short distance away at the edge of the precipice. "Any luck with that treasure?" he asked.

Harold shook his head.

"Me neither," said Mr. Henry. Again, he drew on his cigar, flicking the ash onto the brown stubble. "You know what I think?" he said. He pushed himself closer to where Harold sat. "I think you and me ought to join up."

Harold didn't answer. He seemed not to hear. He was looking over the deep chasm of rocks where the wind continued to blow, noisily now, in frequent abrupt gusts. Mr. Henry touched his arm. Harold recoiled.

"Well, now..." Mr. Henry acted surprised. He looked into Harold's eyes. "You ain't afraid of me, are you?"

Harold stared back at him.

"No. You ain't afraid. We're going to be friends." He put the cigar to his mouth and puffed on it. Then he withdrew and examined it and threw it smoldering into the brush. "Boy like you needs a friend." He nodded.

Harold sat motionless. Mr. Henry reached out and

put a hand on Harold's shoulder. Harold didn't move. "Tell you what," Mr. Henry said, rubbing his fingers gently against Harold's neck. "We won't tell anyone."

The wind gusted fiercely and Harold pulled his head away. Suddenly, he was on his feet. Quick as he could he ran to the other side of the path, beyond the brush, where a flame now was beginning to spread among the dead trees. Mr. Henry stood up. Harold stopped running and the two stood for a moment, unmoving, staring at each other. Then, out of the forest below, echoed the sound of Mr. Davis' voice calling to Harold.

Mr. Henry stepped forward. At that instant the wind whipped through the trees sending a wall of flame high into the sky. Mr. Henry jumped back. The sole of his boot caught a crevice and he fell hard upon his knees. The wind blew with increasing violence, feeding the flames, so that sparks shot out to where Mr. Henry lay. Mr. Henry held onto his knee. His trousers were torn. With some difficulty he rose, and when he was on his feet, he looked past the flames to see Harold watching from the other side of the path. Very carefully, he tried putting weight on his leg. Cautiously, he stepped forward.

Again the wind rose up. Mr. Henry raised his head. The wind hit him full. A look of alarm, then panic raced across his face. For an instant he stood transfixed, staring into the wind. Clouds welled up in the sky above. The fire crackled to the side of him. Gusting, violent blasts beat at him from all directions. Staring fixedly, his arms before his face, he backed away, one step, two steps, and his knee buckled. He reached for his leg, but the piercing noisy wind threw him back. He took another step. The ground gave way beneath his feet. With a wild shriek he went over the edge.

Harold stepped out onto the rock, avoiding the fire.

He looked below. Mr. Davis and Mary were looking up at him. The wind stopped blowing. Clouds continued to gather in the sky. After a moment, the rain began to fall.

Old Route 17 through the Allegany reservation is about as spooky a road as one is ever likely to encounter. Before the interstate opened, the road marked for me the beginning and ending of frequent trips to my home in Connecticut. Arriving usually at dusk on the return trips, I always negotiated old Route 17 with some trepidation. I always held my breath. Today, of course, this is the road less traveled. I am ever thankful to have arrived in Chautauqua County before the opening of the interstate and thus to have become acquainted with old Route 17. So much so that I continue to make an occasional pilgrimage to Salamanca using the old route. "Daniel Kenton" is in the tradition of "The Vanishing Hitchhiker". The reader might consider a visit to old Route 17 after completing the story.

Daniel Kenton

The town of Salamanca was named after the nineteenth century Spanish nobleman who was the principle investor in the railroad that began there, connecting the western Southern Tier with New York City. The railroad crosses land owned by the Seneca Nation of Indians. The town of Salamanca is built on that land. Residents and commercial interests in the town must pay an annual lease fee to the Seneca Nation for the privilege of occupying their land.

To arrive in Salamanca, one must cross the reservation. Today, that is a simple matter. One need only drive East on Interstate 17 from Jamestown and exit at number 21. But it wasn't always that way. Not many years ago, the interstate stopped at the border of the reservation. The Seneca Indians would not allow the white man's highway to pass across their land. To get to Salamanca it was necessary to take a much smaller, two lane road through the forest of the reservation. This road is not only quite hilly, climbing, as it does, the western slopes of the Allegheny foothills; it is also extremely dark. There are few homes or buildings of any kind along its edges. The road follows the curve of the Allegheny River, and often, when the river is sun warmed and the night is cool, the entire area is covered with a dense fog. It is a road one must travel cautiously, because the woods are full of deer. The deer come out at night and often linger by the side of the road. Frequently, they become mesmerized by the headlights of an approaching car. When that happens, they are apt to leap out into the road just as the car is upon them. Many accidents have been caused this way.

About forty years ago there was a country doctor living not too many miles from the reservation outside the pretty little village of Randolph. The doctor's name was Daniel Kenton. He lived in a good old farmhouse with a sturdy old barn on a considerable number of acres. It was the home of his boyhood.

Dr. Kenton was a quiet and serious man, but he hadn't always been that way. As a youth he was handsome and high strung and prone to get what he wanted. He had fair hair then and confident blue eyes. After he became a doctor, he traveled the world and made money. He had lived in cities and been through two wars. And he had loved many women.

Now that he was growing old he had decided to retire and return to the area of his birth, for he remembered the Southern Tier to be a pretty and peaceful country. During his infrequent visits to his family home through the course of his life, folks had always been kind to him and welcomed him; and there were still those left who remembered his mother and father. Word spread quickly after he returned. And soon folks began to call on him and bring him warm food and pies and ask him to take a look at this or that child or ailing husband or wife. There wasn't a great deal of medical help in the country then, so Dr. Kenton soon found himself making regular trips into the village and around the countryside to administer to the sick. He'd take his little black bag and load himself into the big Packard that was his pride and joy and the only luxury he allowed himself from his former days. While he was out traveling the country, he'd look at the beautiful land, the fields and the hills, and try to remember himself here as a young man before he went out into the world.

About this time a new clinic opened up in Salamanca

and he was asked to help staff it. He agreed to work the
emergency room two nights a month. The first time he
drove out was in early April. Darkness was beginning to
fall by the time he reached the little two lane road across
the reservation. It had started to rain, and there were still
patches of snow on either side of the road. He turned up
the heater in the Packard and began to climb the hill
slowly, slowing down even more for the curves. The rain
was coming down pretty hard now, so he moved the windshield wipers on to the high setting. While he crept
along, he was thinking. He remembered having traveled
this road many times before. As a college student he had
often driven out to Salamanca with his friends to drink
beer. And then, he went alone; for there had been a girl.
An Indian girl. What was her name?

He was approaching the crest of the hill now.
Through the rain he could see light moving on the down
side. A car was approaching; too fast, he thought. He
pulled to the right, to the edge of the road, until the two
headlights came up over the hill. The headlights shone in
his eyes, blinding him for a moment. Then they were
gone. For another moment he couldn't see a thing. But
when his vision returned, squinting out through the wet
windshield and the darkness, it seemed as though he saw
movement by the side of the road on the hilltop. Might
he be imagining it? No. There was a figure standing
there in the rain. He drove forward slowly and stopped.
The door of the Packard opened and he felt some of the
cold and the dampness of the night enter, and behind it
the figure of a young woman. She was dark haired, and
her hair was wet. She wore a purple cotton dress with a
string of beads at the neck. As soon as she closed the
door she turned toward Dr. Kenton and looked him full in
the face for what seemed a long time. Then she turned
away and in an even voice said to the doctor, "Please,

could you take me to the bottom of the hill?"

Neither of them spoke as the car moved slowly around the curves. When the road finally flattened out, the young woman spoke again, "Here." Dr. Kenton stopped the car. The rain was still coming down, and there was no sign of a house. Nothing but trees and darkness. "Let me take you to your home." But the young woman was already out and the door closed behind her; and as Dr. Kenton watched, she walked off among the trees and disappeared.

In the days that followed, he thought about her often. She had inspired in him a strange and unfamiliar feeling, almost a dread, but he had also been touched by pity. The weather grew warmer after the rain. The sun came out and warmed the earth, and he began to plan for a vegetable garden. Nights he spent looking over the old books in his father's library. One night he pulled from the shelf a fine old copy of Herman Melville. It was a book his father had given him, he remembered; and it felt comfortable in his hands. Inside, in his father's beautiful script, there was an inscription:

> *To my son, Daniel*
> *On leaving for medical school*
> *September 6, 1912*
> *All my love,*
> *Father*

And then the book seemed to fall open on its own and between the pages he discovered an envelope, a letter of some kind. It was addressed to him. When he picked it up, he felt a little thrill of excitement. He took the letter out of the envelope and opened it carefully. It, too, was dated September 6, 1912. He read:

My Dearest Daniel,
  I am sad tonight. I am happy, too.
I had a dream. I dreamed you came for
me in a big shiny car. You are a doctor.
You will be a fine doctor, my Daniel.
I will wait. My love is always, like the sun.

Rachel

He closed the letter tenderly and replaced it in the envelope. For a moment he held the envelope in his hand, then he returned it to the book and closed the book. *Rachel.* That was her name. That was the name of the Indian girl he went off on the reservation to see. She had loved him. He hadn't remembered that. And he felt shame.

The weather turned again, cold. The day arrived for him to drive again to the clinic in Salamanca. When he turned off the interstate, the hill was covered with fog. He switched his headlights on dim, but as he began to climb the fog got thicker. Darkness began to fall. The light from his headlights reflected off the fog, bathing the road and the trees in a silver glow. Beyond was nothing but darkness. Slowly, he crept up the hill, around the curves. Suddenly, as he turned around a bend, the head-lights fell upon a pair of sparkling eyes. His heart leaped in his chest. It was a deer, a young doe, standing motion-less by the side of the road, staring into the headlights. He slowed almost to a stop. The doe was frozen in panic. He passed within yards of her, and when he was beyond, she bounded off into the woods.

Now he was approaching the top of the hill. He was approaching the spot where he had met the young Indian woman. He strained to see through the fog and the silver glow, and for the first time he began to be afraid. The

silver light danced off the fog. He kept creeping on, forever cautious, until finally he reached the crest of the hill,
and over he went, the headlights shining out through the
dense fog. And then, in some mysterious way, the fog
began to part. A breeze came up, and the fog parted.
This time his heart stopped. There she was. Standing in
the silver glow. Watching the car approach. Waiting.
    He stopped.
    After she was seated inside, she turned to him again
to study his face. Her lips were turned up, just slightly
smiling, and although he was frightened to look at her,
again he felt the touch of pity.
    "Take me to the bottom of the hill."
    He didn't question her. He simply obeyed. He
drove the Packard through the silver fog and the darkness,
downward, in silence, slowly, feeling all the time she was
watching him with that slight smile. And when she said,
"Here!", he stopped again without question; and he
watched while she opened the door and stepped out into
the night and the fog. He watched while she moved off
into the woods, and although he was afraid, he couldn't
bring himself to drive off. Somehow he felt compelled to
sit there, in the big shiny car, and watch through the fog
the young woman who seemed now so familiar. And
now, as he watched, she stopped. She turned and looked
back at him, waiting. He felt his heart beating in his
chest, and then he felt his hand on the door handle; and
almost before he knew what he was doing, he was out of
the car and into the night. The young woman kept
watching him as he stepped into the woods and began to
walk toward her; and then she began to move, too, watching him always, moving backwards through the woods.
Deeper and deeper into the darkness they went, and the
fear kept growing on Dr. Kenton until he could stand it
no longer. He cried out, "No! I won't go any farther."

The woman stopped. She looked him full in the face. From out of the darkness she looked, the smile still on her lips. The cold and the silence of the night chilled his body. The young Indian woman stood motionless, silent, looking at him out of the cold and darkness. He couldn't move. He dared not speak. And then, suddenly, she took a single step in his direction. Not so much as a step, only a movement, a swaying, but it seemed to bring her into a space where there was more light. He felt an urge to turn and run. But now the light was full upon her. The light shone upon her face. He could see her clearly now. She smiled deeper. And with that smile a panic such as he had never known burned cold and numb through the innermost part of his being. *Rachel.* But after the panic he looked again and saw in the face the agony of years of waiting and the weight of betrayal. He managed a whisper, "What do you want?"

She didn't answer. She only raised her arm and pointed. At first he could see nothing. Then, where she was pointing, the light seemed even a little brighter. He stepped forward again and saw that it was a little clearing. The woman moved into the clearing, and he followed. There was a cabin with dim lights at the windows and smoke rising from the chimney. Again, the woman point- ed, this time at the ground. He looked into her face that was surrounded by darkness. The smile was gone. And now what he saw there was pain and sadness; and when he followed her arm to the tip of her finger and then beyond to where she pointed on the ground, he saw there a flat stone rising. On the stone was chiseled:

Rachel Cross
1913

Inside, he felt a chill. He stared at the stone for many minutes. Finally, when he looked up and around, she was gone. As if in a daze he walked around the cabin, having to feel his way in the dark. But she was gone. He was alone in the vast darkness. He stumbled to the cabin door and began to beat upon it. From the force of his blows the door opened. A man stood inside facing him. He was a powerfully built man, neither young nor old. He was holding a wooden spoon. Behind him a fire was burning in the fireplace and a cast iron pot hung over it. The two men looked at each other in silence. After a moment the man stepped toward Dr. Kenton, and almost at the same moment Dr. Kenton stepped into the cabin. Again, they stood looking into each other's face. The man had streaks of yellow in his hair and clear blue eyes. They looked at each other for a long time, and finally the man spoke, as if he had been waiting all those years: "Father?"